T0167619

On Dragonfly Wings may be the least threatening, most touching and thoughtful explorations of past life regression a reader can experience. Starting with the death of her brother, Daniela Norris follows her heart to find what she already intuitively knows: We maintain connections with those we love who have gone before and we will meet again. We have only to listen, and to remember. In this outstanding, concise, easily readable book, Norris provides a remarkable journey into this 'remembering.' She melts the barriers between life and death in a gentle, loving way. Through her experiences, and with tears and laughter, Norris guides us toward our inner selves and helps us remember who we truly are.

Jim PathFinder Ewing, author of *Reiki Shamanism: A Guide to Out-of-Body Healing* **and** *Conscious Food: Sustainable Growing, Spiritual Eating*

Daniela Norris takes the reader, with warmth and grace, into the discovery of another reality. On Dragonfly Wings is an amazing read, very well written, where from the start we know we are in the hands of a trustworthy and sensitive writer. The pages start to turn on their own as if scenes in a dream sequence. Norris is a master at opening doors and explaining what awaits us. She bids us to accompany her on her journey to mediumship. And we are the richer for having been given this opportunity.

Susan Tiberghien, author of *Looking for Gold* **and** *One Year to a Writing Life*

Dragonfly Wings is filled with education, wisdom and hope for everyone who has lost a loved one or needs information to heal their personal grief. Daniela Norris' journey has expanded her own life and will definitely inspire yours. The death of her brother is Daniela's spiritual gain. The ripple effect is that anyone who reads this book will be similarly blessed!

Lo Anne Mayer, author of *Celestial Conversations: Healing Relationships After Death.*

A delightful book that you will find hard to put down once you start to read.

Andy Tomlinson, author of *Healing the Eternal Soul* **and** *Exploring the Eternal Soul*

On Dragonfly Wings

A Skeptic's Journey to Mediumship

On Dragonfly Wings

A Skeptic's Journey to Mediumship

Daniela I. Norris

AXIS MUNDI
BOOKS

Winchester, UK
Washington, USA

First published by Axis Mundi Books, 2014
Axis Mundi Books is an imprint of John Hunt Publishing Ltd., Laurel House, Station Approach,
Alresford, Hants, SO24 9JH, UK
office1@jhpbooks.net
www.johnhuntpublishing.com
www.axismundi-books.com

For distributor details and how to order please visit the 'Ordering' section on our website.

ISBN: 978 1 78279 512 4

A CIP catalogue record for this book is available from the British Library.

Design: Stuart Davies
www.stuartdaviesart.com

Printed and bound by CPI Group (UK) Ltd, Croydon, CR0 4YY

We operate a distinctive and ethical publishing philosophy in all
areas of our business, from our global network of authors to
production and worldwide distribution.

CONTENTS

"Elementary logic requires that, in order to discuss an issue, one should be familiar with it. The opinion of a critic has no value unless they talk about something they know perfectly well."
(Allan Kardec, *Book on Mediums and Evokers*, 1861)

For Michael

Preface

My brother Michael died on a late spring day in May. He was just a week short of twenty. I was thirty-eight. I believe this is when it all started, or perhaps it started some twenty years earlier – or maybe even twenty years before *that* – but I was always told that stories don't necessarily have to start at the beginning. So the question of when it all started becomes futile, especially if you believe in the elasticity of time.

Michael went swimming a week before his twentieth birthday, and drowned. It was a hot Thursday and steam rose from the white sand like an omen from the mouth of an oracle. Pale blue linum flowers withered in the afternoon heat, and he decided to go to the beach with a few of his friends. Michael was tall and strong. In fact, he was on a weekend's leave from the military – my brother was a tank commander. Tank commanders are not the most likely people to drown in the sea on a hot, sunny day. But the sea was rough, and the group chose a spot far away from the lifeguard. Some of the guys went surfing and another fell asleep in the sun. It was Michael and another friend who volunteered to accompany one of the girls who wanted to go in for a dip despite the turbulent waters.

The water was angry and murky, and even though they only went in waist deep, it very quickly turned into a swirly rip current. The girl got out; Michael's friend made it back as well.

Michael didn't.

One

regressing

There are twenty of us in the large room. The ceiling is high and imposing and the large carpet soft and inviting. Some of us are seated on the comfortable sofas that are arranged along the walls, while others sit at the foot of the sofas, on the plush carpet. Four large chandeliers hang over our heads, while we all watch Bob, who lies on a mattress in the middle of the circle we've formed. His eyes are closed, but his eyelids flutter. Even I – being myopic – can see it clearly. And I don't really know if I believe in hypnosis – or in life after death, or in reincarnation for that matter – but I am there, watching with curiosity and a mixture of awe and apprehension.

"Where are you?" asks the man sitting next to him, in a soft voice. This is Andy, our instructor.

"A field," mumbles Bob. "A field, it is dry, very, very dry…"

"Tell me more," says Andy.

Bob is silent for a few moments, as if he is observing something important. People under hypnosis often take a while to respond.

"It hasn't rained for months," says Bob. "We have no food. Everyone's hungry."

"Do you have a family or are you alone?"

"I think I do…yes…a wife, I have a wife. And a small child. They are hungry. I need to find a way to feed them."

Bob is breathing hard, and we cannot take our eyes off his face and his wildly fluttering eyelids. He sees images, images that cause him pain, that affect him deeply. For him, at that very moment, these images are more real than the twenty people sitting in a circle around him. For Bob, we are all thin air at this moment. The dry field, the wife, the hungry child, are real. And

2

he is struggling, struggling with finding a way to get food for them.

"To the count of three, I am going to take you to the next significant event," says Andy. "One, two, three. Where are you now?"

Bob starts crying silently. His lips quiver. We all hold our breaths.

"I am standing by their graves…" he whispers. Some of the people in the circle inch forward, struggling to hear.

"What happened?" asks Andy, his voice low and compassionate.

"I couldn't help them, I couldn't…" whispers Bob, tears rolling down his cheeks. His eyes remain closed.

"What happens next?" asks Andy, and Bob proceeds to describe an uneventful end of a life, which seems to be all about coping with failure, death and grief. It is difficult to watch him struggle with his internal demons, but when Bob is brought back into the here and now, his eyes shine.

"Now I understand," he says. "I understand some things about my current life."

Andy smiles and nods. He doesn't ask Bob to share his insights with the others.

"All we need to know is that Bob has something to work with," Andy says. "This has achieved his session's objective."

We all take a break and gather outside, nursing our warm mugs in our hands. This is rural England, after all, and an afternoon break for a cup of tea on the lawn is part of what one does regularly when attending a past life hypnotic regression course.

Not far from the Dorset coast, in a beautiful old mansion now used as a spiritual retreat center. The Regression Academy runs training courses for Past Life Regression Therapists.

I am now one of the students.

Clutching my cup of tea, I approach Janet, one of the teaching assistants in the course. I've heard she is a talented medium, and I want to ask her about the previous night's events, as they've been on my mind all day.

"Hi, Janet," I say gingerly, not sure how to approach the bizarre question I am about to ask. I am certain that anywhere else such a question would get me some very strange looks, but I have the feeling that I might get away with it here, in this magical estate where the floors creak and the paint on the ceilings peels in long, crumbling strips.

This magnificent place carries a very tangible out-of-this-world quality, one where anything is possible.

"Hi," she says. "How are you doing?"

Janet used to work in Investment Management in London for many years, until one day she'd heard her true calling. She had a natural gift for mediumship and as a child she regularly conversed with spirits and ghosts. Her family wasn't too impressed so she tried to ignore these gifts when she was younger; she even thought of them as a curse at various points in her life. But once she learned how to harness and use her special gift to help others, she abandoned her job in the City and started working as a therapist. She now specializes in releasing dark energies.

"Fine," I say, "really good. I just wanted to ask you about last night…"

Janet smiles, and takes a long sip out of her mug.

Two

bad news travels fast

When someone tells you to call them because they have bad news, you hope that perhaps you didn't hear correctly. Then you hope that maybe it is something relatively minor like a broken arm or a stolen car.

I was in London with my friend Shireen when I got the news of Michael's death. Shireen is Palestinian, I am Israeli – and we've written a book together. It is an exchange of letters between two women on both sides of the Israeli-Palestinian divide. In it we discuss history and politics, but also music, recipes and the education of our children.

We'd been asked by our publisher to come to London to attend a series of events related to the book launch. Although we'd both been to London before and appreciated all the city has to offer, it was the first time we were there as representatives of our respective people and cultures. Truth be told, we never thought of ourselves as representatives of anything. We are simply two women, two mothers, who think that all the fighting and bloodshed are unnecessary: that our two peoples can live together in the same land, and that it is the extremists on both sides who hinder the process. But when you write a book on the subject, you somehow immediately become responsible – in the eyes of many – for every stupid action or unintelligent word from your people and your government. We were just discovering this universal truth, but we did find some time for shopping and socializing between the various literary events and interviews our publisher had organized. Overall, we were having a good time.

When I got that message from my mom, Shireen and I, together with our four-year-old boys Mohammad and Adam, were on a bus near Marble Arch. We'd just finished eating at Wetherspoon's, a local pub chain. It is perhaps not the most obvious place to eat when an Israeli and a Palestinian visit London, but it is a great place to eat when you're dragging a couple of little boys in tow and are desperate for something tasty, quick and affordable. So we ate a huge curry with heaps of white rice, surrendered to the children's requests for a humongous warm chocolate cake with vanilla ice cream and then got onto the bus to go back to our hotel.

The red double-decker bus struggled through the afternoon rush-hour traffic, inching its way among taxis and cars driven by people keen to get back home and start the weekend. Adam and Muhammad sat like two little statues, which was not at all typical of them – they are the kind of boys who'd normally be spotted climbing on chairs, emptying out the cupboards or rearranging the furniture.

But they were fascinated by what went on around them – the people, the colors, the foreign landscape of a bustling city in a pre-weekend frenzy. I smiled at Shireen, recognizing the shared pleasure of a few moments of relative quiet for two mothers who've just had a hectic week. We'd already agreed a long time ago that the things we shared were greater than the things that divided us, even if without any doubt those latter existed. I then peeked at my mobile phone. There was a missed call from my mom, and a message on the answering system.

It is strange how certain events in life get broken down into the 'befores' and the 'afters'. 'Before' things are as they are, no more and no less than what you experience at a certain moment and then forget. The 'after', or that specific 'after', was the afternoon of a sticky day in late May. It was my mom's strained voice that sounded in my ear, with the background of white noise of people, cars, passengers on the bus.

She said, "Call home as soon as you can, I've got bad news."

"I have a ninety-five-year-old grandmother, a wonderful

stepdad who underwent heart surgery last month and a brother who is a soldier. Who do you think it is?" I asked Shireen, already feeling the beginning of a lump in my throat and a pain in my stomach.

"Don't think like this," she said. "Maybe it's something else."

I normally trust Shireen's analysis of things, but even she didn't look convinced.

We waited until the bus spat us out on a busy street dotted with Middle-Eastern restaurants, and I ducked into the entrance of one of them to dial my mom's number. Shireen grabbed the two little boys by the hand and took a few steps back.

While I pressed the keys slowly, the smell of deep fried falafel drifted towards me, and it made me feel sick. My mom picked up the phone on the third ring.

"I don't know how to tell you this," she said in a strained voice. I took a deep breath.

"What is it, Mom?"

"Michael drowned."

I didn't dare exhale, but then I had to.

"Drowned? What do you mean 'drowned'?"

This didn't make any sense, or maybe it did but my mind refused to accept the two words – a subject and a verb – that formed an entire sentence; a sentence that was about to rock my world. They just didn't connect together – "Michael" and "drowned". After all, Michael was a soldier. Soldiers don't drown, do they? They get killed, they get bombed, they get shot. They even get kidnapped in certain parts of our mad world. But drown? This was surely some kind of mistake.

Later Shireen told me that as soon as she heard it was my brother, she just hoped it did not have anything to do with 'them' – with Palestinians. She knew that my brother was a solider in the Israeli army and felt ambivalent about this fact. On one hand, this was her good friend's little brother. On the other, he was part of what she always referred to as 'The Occupation Forces'. She could deal with me being Israeli, a civilian (she managed to push the fact that I am a former officer in The Occupation Forces out of her mind – most of the time), but that I had a brother who was a soldier – that was a different story altogether. But now he was gone – even if it still felt as if it couldn't be part of reality, not just yet, and I was stuck in London at the end of a book tour with a friend who was not just any friend, but one who some people would consider to be my enemy. This 'enemy' threw her arms around me and helped me get through that first sleepless night.

Anyone who has experienced the sudden loss of a loved one knows that the first night is the most surreal. All the thoughts that rush into your head and prevent you from sleeping bang against each other like a bag of pebbles, creating so much chatter and noise that make it impossible to sleep.

Finally, in the early hours of the morning when my exhaustion forced me into the comforting arms of temporary oblivion, I surrendered, only to wake up a few short hours later with the new reality hitting me with the impact of a car crash.

Somehow, I managed to get through that night and through the next day before I got the first available flight to Tel Aviv.

Three

goodbyes

I have not lived in Tel Aviv for nearly twenty years now, but in my mind, it is still my home base. This city of upmarket cafés and sleazy nightclubs, of golden beaches and twenty-four-hour shops and restaurants that compete with each other for the clientele that roams around the city streets at dawn looking for something to eat or a place to have a last drink before going to bed, is still my favorite city in the entire world.

True, it is pretentious and ambitious, at once both relaxing and exhausting – but it is *my* city, where I spent my teenage years drifting through the streets and dreaming, window shopping and enjoying the beaches, and my early adulthood years exploring the nightlife and working for my first hard-earned cash that allowed me to study and later to travel the world.

When the plane lands at Ben Gurion airport, I feel that despite all those years of living far away, in Africa, South America and Europe, I've arrived back where everything seems familiar.

It is my mother and stepfather who wait for me at the airport, their faces gray, their shoulders hunched. They take me home, where everything looks the same, yet feels very, very different from my previous biannual visits.

Throughout the confusion and numbness that accompany the departure of a loved one, I wander in a dream-like state. Michael's mates from the military arrive in groups of threes and fours, as if their togetherness is a shield against their sadness, a strategy to cope with their shock.

They look like head-shaved teenagers, which is what they really are. Some still have teenage pimples on their faces. Despite serving as soldiers in the Israeli Army, for many of them this is their first real encounter with death.

9

Then the teachers arrive. First Michael's high-school teacher. Then the teachers from primary and secondary school. My parents' small front room is suddenly more crowded than the central bus station.

I suppose that one advantage of dying so young is that there are a lot of people around to mourn you. I still remember that my great-grandmother, who died at the age of ninety-six, took her last journey accompanied by a handful of relatives, for we are a small family. None of her friends outlived her.

Michael, on the other hand, is the first to depart, and dozens of people pass through my parents' apartment like a stream of dazed butterflies. Looking at the wide-eyed faces of Michael's young friends, I think that the feeling of immortality that twenty-year-olds often experience is like a conglomeratic cliff, which is made up of loosely cemented pebbles and rock, and appears to be solid and eternal. Then a small earthquake hits, and it crumbles into stone and sand.

And these tough soldiers – young men and women – do crumble before my eyes. They sit on the two matching sofas in my parents' front room for hours, staring at nothing in particular and saying nothing in particular, a permanent look of disbelief on their faces.

When a friend of Shireen's, whom I met not long ago, a Palestinian, calls to offer his condolences, the look of disbelief on the faces of Michael's young friends only intensifies. A Palestinian? Calling to offer his condolences for the death of an Israeli soldier? Can this be true or is it just a cruel joke? I assure them it is not a joke. I know the guy. I've met him several times. He really means it.

I, too, feel numb, but my eyes are dry. Something inside me does not let me sink into the same state of despair that seems to envelope others.

I've always been fascinated by the question of where people go after they die. For as long as I can remember, I felt that there must be more than just our body – perhaps a soul that continues beyond physical death. I was never a religious person. If anything, organized religion has always put me off. However, I've always been a spiritual person, convinced that there is more to us than our physical bodies. I'd even had some conversations along those lines with Michael some years back, and now I contemplate these conversations, as if they were important fragments of our relationship. He – teenaged Michael – didn't seem to think the concept was outrageous. But he didn't think that it made much sense either.

"Perhaps when we die someone just pulls the plug," he once said. "And then the show is over. But it's also possible that there's a God after all," he added. "Maybe I'll pray to Him once in a while, just in case."

So here I am, sitting among mourning relatives and friends, and feeling strangely aware of another reality. There is something familiar about this situation – almost as if I knew this unexpected death was going to happen – as if I've dreamt about it and forgot the dream. Almost as if this is a déjà-vu, a situation I've experienced before on some level, and now it is repeating itself. I wonder if grief has messed up with my mind: whether the sadness, the mourning and the overwhelming sense of loss make me imagine things that do not exist. I accept this as a possibility – but no matter how much I try to rationalize it, the feeling of déjà-vu is still there.

When mourning, people often do not know what to say or do. It helps when someone can see a positive in the engulfing negative around them. So I do my best to comfort others, to tell them that perhaps there is a reason for things that happen the way they do. I get strange looks from some, appreciative nods from others.

Then, in the middle of the night, I realize what it is that keeps me from sinking into despair.

I sleep in Michael's room, which used to be my own room

when I lived at home. I left home at the age of twenty, after my military service, and moved to a shared flat close to the Tel Aviv University. Two-year-old Michael, who slept until then in the enclosed, converted terrace, moved into my old room. Now I have my room back, but sleep escapes me.

As I lie awake, listening to the noises of the night coming from the street below my parents' apartment, I feel that my brother is not really gone. I feel that Michael is still here.

Hesitantly, I try to talk to him. I suppose that many people who've lost someone dear to them have talked to them, saying things they have not said when they still could. But the surprising thing for me is not that I talk to Michael. What surprises me that night is that I can hear Michael's answers clearly in my head.

"Are you really dead?" I ask him.

"I don't know," he says. "I think so."

The voice in my head is clear. But many people have been put in straightjackets for having heard voices, so I am not ready to accept or admit – even to myself – what is happening. It feels natural and shocking at the same time.

"Am I going mad?" I ask, and the question is directed both at myself and at Michael.

"No," I immediately hear the answer in my head, even before I finish asking the question. "We are really having this conversation. I am here."

Michael, too, is baffled by what has happened to him; he doesn't understand what exactly is going on. Yet he is calm; he is not afraid. He reassures me that all is well, and this makes me feel better. I finally fall asleep, and wake up the next morning feeling as if something magical had happened to me during the night.

"It was probably all a dream," I say to myself as the day progresses and I contemplate the idea. However, the warm feeling inside stays with me throughout the day, and the optimism that my nightly encounter with Michael has wrapped me in doesn't fade away.

In those few days following Michael's death, I was indeed worried that I was losing my sense of reality. Those days represented my first real encounter with human mortality, the first close death of someone younger than me. I was surprised by how strange it all felt – painful yet familiar. It almost felt as if it were meant to be, although my logical mind kept pointing out to me that no death of a twenty-year-old should be treated as if it were meant to be.

I had experienced the death of my beloved grandparents some ten years back, but it was not as shocking as the death of a twenty-year-old boy, of my little brother. When my grandfather died I was in my late teens, and I sort of tried not to think about it too much. It was too upsetting.

I attended his funeral, and then focused on keeping my grandmother company whenever I could, and spent as much time with her as possible.

When my grandmother died some ten years later, I was in my late twenties, and I continued having conversations with her for many years following her passing. But my conversations with her were very different. She'd show up in my dreams once in a while, as if keeping a prescheduled appointment, and I'd wake up in the morning feeling as if I'd spent the night with her. But this was different. My brother was actually...still here. I could feel his presence, I could hear his thoughts.

Shortly after the news of Michael's death got around, friends and acquaintances started posting on his Facebook page. It quickly filled with words of love, of grief, of condolence. As I scrolled down the page and read these comforting words, I could feel Michael standing behind me.

"I want to read this," he said in my head, and not knowing if this could possibly be true, I left the page open on the screen, just in case.

I knew that if I dared voice any of the above in a room full of grieving relatives and friends, I'd be getting worried glances.

"The poor woman," they would have surely said. "The grief and the shock have messed with her mind."

And this might be true. But for a reason unknown to me, or at least unknown back then, I was certain that Michael was not completely gone. That the plug had not been pulled. That he was still there.

Four

the funeral

The funeral and the hours that followed swam past me like a school of fish in murky water. Hundreds of people in khaki uniform gathered at the military cemetery near Tel Aviv to accompany Michael's coffin. Michael was a soldier when he died and so was given a military funeral – a certain relief for my parents as they did not have to organize a thing.

Obituaries were read by his commander in the army – a young lieutenant with two bars on his shoulders – and by my stepdad Ramy. I was also asked to prepare a few words, but the words didn't come easily. Then, I decided to translate and read from a poem I'd heard once, titled "Death is Nothing at All", by Canon Henry Scott Holland.

Death is nothing at all, I have only slipped away
into the next room.
I am I,
and you are you;
whatever we were to each other,
that, we still are.
Call me by my old familiar name,
speak to me in the easy way
which you always used,
put no difference in your tone,
wear no forced air
of solemnity or sorrow.
Laugh as we always laughed
at the little jokes we shared together.
Let my name ever be
the household word that it always was.

Let it be spoken without effect,
without the trace of a shadow on it.
Life means all
that it ever meant.
It is the same as it ever was.
There is unbroken continuity.
Why should I be out of mind
because I am out of sight?
I am waiting for you,
for an interval,
somewhere very near,
just around the corner.
All is well.

This poem (quoted here in full with the kind permission of Souvenir Press, UK, ISBN-13 978-0285628243, 1987 £4.99) more than anything else, summarizes how I felt in those first days after Michael's death.

Those who've lost a loved one to sudden death can surely understand this deep sense of shock, this elasticity of time that makes the minutes seem like hours and the hours like brief and elusive seconds.

The night after the funeral I lie awake and talk to Michael again.

"I feel that you are here," I say.

"I am," he replies. I cannot really hear his voice, but I can *sense* it. It feels like someone talking to me inside my own head, but it is his voice, his thoughts, not my own.

"No one can hear me, no one but you," Michael adds.

"I can, I can really hear you," I say. He smiles a non-physical smile, a sort of warm feeling of contentment; I also sense he is still a little apprehensive; he is not quite sure what is going on. Neither am I.

Then I fall asleep, because soon it is daylight and I go

downstairs to join my stepfather, Ramy, Michael's father, who looks as if he hasn't slept a moment.

"I dreamt of Michael," I tell him. I lack better words, for I don't know how to explain what really happened.

He sighs.

"I feel he is still with us," I say.

He looks up at me, his eyes full of tears.

"If only it were true," he says.

It was Plato who said that we can easily forgive a child who is afraid of the dark, but the real tragedy of life is when men are afraid of the light. At that moment, the light for me is a new, parallel reality I'd just found – a reality where perhaps death is not the end, but the beginning of something different, some kind of life in a parallel dimension. I feel it as strongly as someone feels love or regret or sadness – not tangible, not measurable, but very physical nonetheless. Am I afraid of it? I ask myself. Should I be? Should I worry about what people say and think of me if I voice my thoughts?

"It is," I say. "It is true, Ramy. He *is* here, I can feel it with clarity. Not only at night, but even at this very moment."

Ramy drops his head in his hands and says nothing. I can feel Michael standing close to us.

Five

first connections

So how did I find myself at a past life regression course in rural England?

I've always considered myself a pretty rational person – one that believes that there is something beyond everyday life but feels uncomfortable with organized religion.

Something has changed since Michael's death. Since he died, I've experienced a contact with what seemed to be a world beyond ours almost on a daily basis. The number of incidents where I just knew things were going to happen – and they did – or knew things about other people, often complete strangers, increased tenfold.

Despite initial fears that perhaps I was losing my mind as a result of the shock and grief my brother's death had caused me, or perhaps because of these initial fears, I decided to try and learn more about the world beyond ours.

As a result of a series of what most people would call coincidences, I ended up taking a basic hypnosis course, and then I'd signed up for this year-long hypnotic regression therapy course. I was now training to become a Past Life Regression Therapist – not because I believed that past lives actually existed, but because I was curious to find out more about this possibility.

Gaunts House isn't very far from the small towns of Christchurch and Poole in Dorset County. On the first evening, after dinner and an introductory meeting where everyone says a few words about who they are and why they've come here, we get ready to go to our assigned rooms. When Hazel, the co-instructor, asks who is willing to be a fire angel – to make sure everyone on their floor is awake in case of a fire alarm going off – I volunteer. After all, I've been in the military for nearly three years and am used to jumping up in the middle of the night in case of necessity, plus – when does the fire alarm ever go off in the middle of the night anyway?

Well, that night it does.

It shakes me out of my sleep and I jump out of bed, adrenaline pumping. I look down, checking that I look more or less respectable and rush into the corridor. I start banging on doors.

"Wake up, wake up," I call out. "The fire alarm went off."

Everyone trickles out of their rooms, in pajamas, dressing gowns and – those who are very quick at getting dressed – jeans and t-shirts. All these people, who met only the evening before, gather in the corridor in the middle of the night, looking at each other's tired faces in wonder. We pause. We wait a moment or two. There is no smell of smoke. No sign of fire. No sense of panic. What is going on? As we start down the stairs, one of the staff comes up and tells us to go back to our beds.

"It's a false alarm," he says.

"At least we got a bonding experience," someone says and the others chuckle.

"Good night," says someone else. "See you in the morning."

We all go back to our rooms, hoping for no more disturbances for the rest of the night.

As I lie in bed under the thin blanket in the warm early-June night, I have a feeling that it will not be over that quickly. In the months to follow I would learn to trust these feelings, but at that early stage I was not quite there yet.

However, it didn't matter what I was feeling or thinking, for one way or another, within ten minutes or so, the fire alarm goes off again.

This time I am awake, so it takes me ten seconds to be out of the room and in the corridor again, banging on doors.

"Fire alarm…" I call out, somewhat less enthusiastically than the previous time.

People shuffle their feet towards the stairs. No one feels like going down and out, into the late-spring night.

"Is this a joke?" someone says and I have the distinct feeling that indeed, it might be. It feels as if someone is trying to play a trick on us.

And I do something that I would not have dared do in any other circumstance. But a gathering in the middle of the night with a small group of strangers in their pajamas, in the corridor of a mysterious old house, is not an everyday situation. So I take off my necklace – that has a small agate locket on it – and say, "Shall we find out?"

I can't logically explain why I did that, for I am not one of those people who regularly use a pendulum to find out what the weather will be like next week. Neither do I ask about the gender of a baby in a friend's bump or the outcome of the weekly lotto. But I do own a pendulum, and I had started using it a few months before this nightly encounter, after reading an article about pendulums in a spiritual and natural living magazine.

I then started practicing on everything and anything around me. Turned down cards? No problem, I tried to guess what they were. Lost keys? The pendulum was out, and to my great surprise I often did indeed guess the right numbers and shapes on the card or found my keys.

This increased my confidence in the power of pendulum work, although I suspect it did so at the cost of losing one or two friends who started labeling me as 'weird' and kept their distance.

However, in this dark corridor in the middle of the night, the eyes of a group of strangers light up immediately. For people who come to a past life regression course are usually open to mystical experiences, are they not?

Again, there was no sign of smoke, no sign of fire, and this time round – no sign of any of the Gaunts House staff.

"Where are our instructors, anyway?" wonders Paul aloud and I realize that indeed, Andy, Hazel, and even Janet, the teaching assistant – who would have been the perfect people to deal with what might be a dark energy waking us in the middle of the night – were nowhere to be seen.

I straighten the silver chain and let the stone locket hang, waiting for any motion to cease.

The way a pendulum works is a curious one, for no one knows exactly where the answers come from, but the surprising thing is that one way or another, answers do come. Some say they come from a higher source, others say they come from a 'higher self', yet others say that the movement is achieved by involuntary and minor movement of the finger muscles.

Skeptics will, of course, turn their noses up at this interesting exercise, but this is probably because they've never personally witnessed a pendulum session.

When the person holding the pendulum holds it by the attached chain, between their pointing finger and thumb, and asks a question, the pendulum moves in one predetermined direction – say, clockwise – for a positive answer, and in the other direction for a negative answer. A pendulum may give a positive or negative answer, or sometimes it may give no answer at all, dangling stubbornly and silently. The latter rarely happens, but when it does, it might be because the question that was asked was not clear enough, or because it cannot be answered at that specific moment, for one reason or another.

So here I am, holding my pendulum, and experiencing mild performance anxiety mixed with excitement. I've used the pendulum many times on my own; but now, here is this group of people whom I only met last night, staring at me and at the pendulum in my hand.

I take a deep breath, and try to still my hand and clear my mind, the first two rules when handling a pendulum.

"May I ask some questions?" I start. One of the things that

I've learned a while back is that when dealing with people in our world or spirits in the worlds beyond ours (for they are not that different from one another) it is always best to be polite and respectful. I wait, and hold my breath. I make sure my fingers don't move, and hold my hand as still as I can. A slow, hesitant movement starts to occur in the pendulum, and then its speed increases. The pendulum circles clockwise, which means 'yes'.

"Is this alarm because of a real fire?" I ask, and wait. Clockwise is my agreed positive reply, programmed when I first started using this pendulum some months back. Every pendulum needs to be 'programmed' by its handler to give an agreed upon direction for each answer. Now the pendulum turns counter-clockwise, meaning 'no'. OK, so apparently, there's no real fire.

"Did someone make this fire alarm go off twice now?" I ask. Everyone stares at my pendulum. A confident clockwise swing is immediately recognizable. The pendulum then comes to a stand-still.

"Is this someone here now?" I ask. Positive answer again.

"Are you doing this to annoy us?" I ask. The pendulum starts turning counter-clockwise, for 'no'.

I think for a few moments. The pendulum comes to a stand-still again, as if waiting for my next question. An idea pops into my mind. Often, the pendulum answers as soon as the idea forms in the handler's mind, but nonetheless, I ask the question out loud.

"Are you lonely?"

The pendulum is already turning clockwise. 'Yes'.

"Are you a woman?" I ask, careful to ask the question in such a way that a 'yes' or 'no' answer will be easy to interpret.

The pendulum turns clockwise – 'yes' again.

"That's really cool," someone says, and the others smile.

"If we go back to sleep will the fire alarm go off again?" I continue.

The pendulum turns clockwise immediately, and everyone

laughs.

I look at the faces around me, and am surprised to realize that I feel instant warmth and friendship towards this group of strangers. These are people whom I've just met, and yet I am able to connect with them on a very profound level. I am able to be myself with them, to do something that I would not dream of doing with any of my family or friends back home. They would think I'd gone mad. While these people – they just think that this is all so natural, so normal.

"What now?" I ask the smiling faces around me.

"I am going to bed," says Paul. "Good night."

Paul is a tall man, in his early fifties. He is the only one who somehow manages to emerge from his room fully clothed, complete with jeans, buttoned up shirt and polished shoes with properly tied laces. And off he goes, back to his room. The rest of us hesitate.

"Ask her if she'd like us to stay with her a little longer," suggests Lorraine, a long-haired woman who already works as a hypnotherapist, and came to this course because she wanted to delve deeper into the world of past life regression.

"Would you like us to stay here with you and keep you company for a while longer?" I ask, and the pendulum turns clockwise almost immediately. 'Yes'.

Everyone around me smiles again. So we seem to have a friendly, lonely ghost on our hands.

"What now?" I ask my new friends, and they shrug.

"I guess we wait," says Lorraine. We do for a while, until one by one the small crowd starts yawning, and one by one they head back to their rooms. Finally it is just Lorraine and me, sitting on the stairs between the dark corridors of floors two and three.

"Let's just go back to bed," I say. Lorraine agrees. Perhaps it is all a figment of my imagination anyway, I think to myself. No point in spending the night out here in the corridor, especially as we have a long day of studies starting in less than four hours.

Back in my room, I sit on the bed and look around me. I am reluctant to go back to sleep as I sense there is a good chance of being woken up again. Besides, I feel excited and curious, and yes, also a little afraid. What is really going on here? It feels as if I am in some kind of dream, or if not a dream, at least a parallel reality.

I turn my attention to my room. It is sparsely furnished – three wooden single beds with thin mattresses, three night tables, two chairs and one chest of drawers. It is meant for sharing, and the empty space around me feels even emptier as I scan the white walls and the single sink in the corner. The toilets are down the hall, and I regret not having visited them earlier, when everyone else was around. Now I don't feel like facing the long, dark corridor on my own, so I lie in bed fully awake. When I signed up for the course, I paid a small extra to have a room to myself, because I like my privacy, and I also like to read and write at night. Back home, I often wake up at 4 am and work for an hour or two. I did not want to inflict this nocturnal restlessness on anyone sharing a room with me. Now I begin to wonder whether this was a good idea.

I keep my bedside light on and try to read, but I am too restless, too distracted. I see shadows everywhere. I wish I wasn't alone.

I leave the small light on, and close my eyes. My hearing sharpens as I do that. The room is perfectly still, and yet I can feel a presence. I have no way of knowing if this is my imagination or if there's anything really there – but I don't have to wait long and wonder. Just a few moments later, the fire alarm goes off again.

I get out of bed, this time slowly, taking my time to put on a cardigan and get a drink of water. I am thinking that this time, it might take a while before we all go back to sleep. It is obvious that we cannot continue through the night like this.

I don't have to knock on any doors this time; everyone walks out into the corridor, rubbing their eyes.

"So what do we do?" I ask.

We start brainstorming. Some of the people in the group have done energy work before. Heather, a small and delicate-looking Canadian woman, says she can sense energies. This is not a bad thing if you believe you might be dealing with a body-less entity. I am still not sure how I feel about all this. Part of me just knows there is something beyond everyday reality. Another part of me doubts – how do I know this is for real?

Heather starts walking along the corridor with her hands sensing the air in front of her.

"Yes, I can sense something here," she says. She advances along the corridor, and then walks back, her hands moving in circular motions. I can see nothing and I can sense nothing, but I bear with her. What she does looks very strange to me – can you really use your hands as energy sensors, I wonder. Maybe Heather is bluffing – but why would she?

"I can sense her," she says, "she is here. She is very agitated."

"Let's help her go up to the light," says Lorraine.

'The Light' is a pretty common expression in these circles, so no one bats an eyelid when it is used. 'The Light' refers to the God-like entity, also sometimes called The Source. Few people in these circles talk about God, for this word has come to be too closely associated with organized religion, with politics and with historic and current religious wars.

I, too, feel uncomfortable with the term 'God' as I've always thought of myself as non-religious. However, the terms The Source of Everything, or even The Light, have a strangely positive affect on me. These are terms I can live with, that don't make me feel uncomfortable.

Many believe that everything comes from one single source, and we all eventually go back to this source of energy. This might be the same God that so many religions talk of, but instead of being an omniscient entity that records every action every single human being is doing for later use in order to filter us into Heaven or Hell, this Source actually encourages us to experiment. Those who believe in reincarnation (about twenty percent of the seven billion people currently living on earth) think that we are coming here, into this world, again and again, as different people, different genders and to different situations, until we have learned everything there is to learn here. Then, when we've been through the different stages and developed our soul, we can achieve 'enlightenment' – and join the Source again.

What I like about this belief is that it makes people look for a big picture, and think more about how they behave in this life and what they achieve, as it might influence their next lives. I also like another aspect of it: that negative experiences teach us as much as positive experiences do; sometimes they teach us more.

But a somewhat unsettling conclusion of the above is that we continue to exist as energies even after we die, and between our earth-lives. Body-less energies such as the one that was now apparently wandering the corridor, agitated.

"So how do we send her back to the Source?" I ask Lorraine.

"Let's all hold hands," she says confidently. "Then we have to imagine her going up and out of here, to the light."

We form a circle, hold hands, and close our eyes. No further words are needed, for each of us seems to know what we have to do. I imagine a portal, a kind of opening high up above, that leads to the spirit realm. I envisage a bright light shining through it, a light that would signal to this entity where it needs to go. I try to focus on that light in my mind's eye. A few moments later we open our eyes and look at each other.

"I think we can go back to bed now," says Heather.

We all do. And the fire alarm does not go off again for the rest of our stay at Gaunts House.

The following day, when asked, Janet told me she was in her room together with Hazel, talking to an earth-bound energy in order to move her on. *It was a female energy,* said Janet, *and she was just lost and lonely.* The feeling of confirmation – that I sensed the same thing as Janet on my very first night at Gaunt's House – was eerie.

How To 1: using a pendulum

Using a pendulum is perhaps the easiest skill to learn if you'd like to start exploring realities beyond our own. All you need to do is suspend your disbelief for twenty minutes, and find a simple chain you could use.

Any chain with a pendant or locket hanging from it will do, although if you start using it regularly you might consider making or buying a special pendulum. To start with, even a key on a simple chain can work; so experiment with something you have around the house before you decide to invest in personal crystal pendulum.

Sit quietly and take a few deep breaths to relax your mind; then try to empty it from thoughts. Sometimes it helps to just focus on your breathing – in, out, in, out.

Imagine a protective bubble of white light around you, through which only the purest energies can pass, and ask for your higher self or for a spirit guide to allow you to communicate. Imagine you are a hollow pipe, just a body that can transfer information without interfering with it. Easier said than done, I know. But still, with practice it will become easy.

Hold the chain between your thumb and pointing finger, and ask the pendulum out loud to show you a 'yes' answer. Wait for a few moments – and observe the motion of the pendulum. Sometimes it will move in a circle, at other times it will move away from you and towards you or from right to left. Each pendulum is different. Once you've established what is considered a 'yes', ask for a 'no' answer.

Now you are ready to start asking questions – but start with easy ones, and follow Three Basic Rules:

1   Always ask a question which can be answered by a 'yes' or a 'no'

2 Don't ask about the future – at least not until you are comfortable with using a pendulum and understand that there are many possible futures, each with its own path.

3 Don't ask questions that you're emotionally involved with until you learn to control your emotions – or they might influence the answer!

A few examples for questions you could start with:

1 Am I a man?
2 Am I a woman?
3 Am I wearing a green shirt?
4 Am I wearing blue trousers?
5 Did I just eat lunch?

It might seem silly to use a pendulum to answer such questions, but it isn't. It is a way to build confidence in the answers the pendulum is giving you – and to communicate with your higher self. Do not use the pendulum – at least in the beginning – to make major decisions. Trust your inner voice before you trust the pendulum.

The next step would be to use the pendulum to answer questions for other people – questions you are not emotionally involved in. Sit with a friend and let them ask the questions – just instruct them to follow the three basic rules above. At this stage, you can also probably try to guess the gender of an unborn baby – a favorite among novice pendulum users.

As you gain experience and confidence in using a pendulum, you can use it to make everyday decisions. Always remember: it is just a tool to help you connect to your inner voice, or higher self. As you advance on your spiritual journey, you'll be able to trust this inner voice without needing 'external' or 'visual' aids. Have fun, and never take it too seriously. A spiritual journey should be a positive and enjoyable experience!

Using a pendulum: quick guide

1 Find an object you can hang on a chain, or use a crystal pendulum if you have one.
2 Sit quietly and take a few deep breaths. Try to empty your mind from thoughts, and focus on your breathing to help you do so.
3 Imagine a protective bubble of white light around you, through which only the purest energies can pass.
4 Ask your higher self, or a spirit guide, to guide you and communicate with you.
5 Ask the pendulum to show you a 'yes' answer, and a 'no' answer. Accept that some questions cannot be answered at the moment, for various reasons.
6 Start by asking simple 'yes' or 'no' questions in which there are no emotion involved, such as: Am I a man? Am I a woman? Am I wearing a blue shirt?
7 As you progress and practice, and learn to control your emotions and thoughts, you can ask more difficult questions.
8 Practice by asking 'yes' or 'no' questions for friends.
9 End the session by thanking your Higher Self, or you Spirit Guide, for their assistance and communication.

Six

before and after

It would not be an overstatement to say that the first regression course has completely changed the way I look at life. However, this change was not something completely unfamiliar; it felt more like a homecoming.

When I was as young as four or five, I would wake up in the middle of the night, and feel that the air around me was thick and heavy. I often felt completely disconnected from my body, sometimes even looking at it from above. I could go back into it at will, and then I'd lie awake in bed, moving my hands and feet to make sure I was not dreaming. I would listen to the sounds of the night around me – a passing car, a barking dog. There was no fear in those moments. I would wonder about the sensations I was experiencing, but then a calming presence would wash over me and I'd fall back to sleep. And I didn't think much of it, for I was certain everyone experiences these night-time shifts of consciousness. Then these experiences went away and I more or less forgot about them.

Like many people, I've asked myself existential questions. While other teenage girls were busy with makeup and clothes, I found time for various esoteric activities such as tarot card reading, palm reading and other forms of divination. These were an integral part of who I was at sixteen (although I'd be lying if I said that makeup and fashionable clothes were completely absent from my list of priorities).

Around that age I discovered the Emin – a group that is today known as The Template Foundation – through my very first love. His name was Tal, and he was a couple of years older than me, and very spiritual. I am not sure if this is what I was attracted to – of course, he was also handsome, intelligent, and *two years older,* which as a teenager is most exciting. He took me along to Emin meetings, and there I found many kinder spirits – people of all ages who were interested in what lies beyond our everyday lives. From where I stand today, I can identify these Emin meetings as my first earthly bridge to the spirit world. I can also identify Tal's role in my life, which went way beyond the importance that a first love carries. I later learned that some people act as 'flags' in your life, they draw your attention to things that you wouldn't have noticed otherwise. Then they can stay in your life, or sometimes drift away – like Tal did. I was not spiritual enough for him, and he broke up our nearly two-year-long relationship. It was not for another young woman or for lack of love for me – he had simply decided to dedicate his time to more spiritual matters. Today I can understand this, but back then, at age seventeen, I was heartbroken. Perhaps this was something that pushed me away from spirituality for a while – after all, spirituality had won the competition over Tal's heart.

Back to 'flags', for today I can recognize their presence and importance in my life; in fact, people who act as 'flags' are present in everyone's life, and they are not always aware of their own important role. This role is to help us get on a certain path, which will serve to advance us on our particular quests. Tal was definitely such a 'flag' for me.

My mother adored him – for he was a quiet, polite and respectful young man – but she did not like the Emin. When trying to find out where her teenage daughter was going on weekends, she'd heard some talk of this spiritual organization being some kind of sect. She was worried that it might be the kind of place where people were brainwashed and cleared of their worldly possessions. Of course, being seventeen, I didn't possess much more than a few pairs of torn jeans, and when I pointed out to her that at least I didn't experiment with sex or drugs like many other young people, I was able to put her mind at ease for a while. I tried to tell her a little about these meetings, which included many hours of spiritual teachings and quiet meditation, but at the time I felt that she could not relate to such things.

At the Emin I was taught to see auras – the subtle energy bodies that surround all living things – people, animals and plants. I was skeptic at first – why would anyone have something so surreal surrounding their bodies, something that cannot be seen with the naked eye? Well, it was a surprise to realize that the aura *can* be seen with the naked eye. And anyone can see it – if they look in the right place and take the time to practice.

How To 2: seeing auras

People can see auras in different ways, but one of the easiest methods to start is to ask a like-minded friend, who doesn't mind experimenting, to sit with their back to a white wall.

Make sure the lights are not too bright and that the phone is off the hook. It is best to turn off your mobile phone as well, as the radiation from a mobile phone can actually shrink the size of a person's aura (see How To 7).

Stand or sit quietly about three meters (ten feet) from your friend and take a few deep breaths. Then focus on your friend's forehead, more or less at the third-eye area – just above the space between the eyebrows. Slowly you might start noticing a white halo-like light that is visible around the person's head.

With time and practice, you might see it around people's heads and bodies in different situations. With even more time and practice, you might start seeing colors in the aura.

To practice aura gazing, you need to be in a quiet place, and remain focused. Once you are out in the 'real world', it is hard to find that place of stillness inside you that allows you to see auras – so no worries, it is very unlikely that anyone can see your aura while you are queuing at the post office.

The thing is, once you start looking for auras around people's heads and bodies, you are more or less on a one-way street – heading towards discoveries that will change the way you think about everyday life.

Seeing auras: quick guide

1 Ask a friend to sit or stand in front of a white wall.
2 Turn off mobile phones, and dim the lights.
3 Sit or stand still in front of your friend, about three meters (ten feet) away.
4 Take a few deep breaths, and focus on your friend's

forehead – at the 'third eye' area.

5 After a few moments, you might notice a halo-like white
light around their head or shoulders.

6 With time and practice, you might be able to see the larger
aura, which can be quite a few feet wide. You might even
be able to notice colors within the aura.

When other parents and family members got worried about their
loved ones spending more and more time with the Emin crowd,
a meeting was organized and some teachings were presented.
The objective was to show anyone interested that we were not
some kind of secret society or soul-grabbing sect. The emphasis
was on personal and spiritual development and the instructors
(or guides, as we used to call them) presented workshops that
dealt with colors, body language and also – not to disappoint
those who were expecting some bizarre happenings at the Tel
Aviv Emin center – there were aura watching and tarot card
reading sessions.

This was a 'light' version of spirituality, which even my mom
could live with. Her worries somewhat subsided after she went
to that meeting together with my stepdad, Ramy, but they were
both quite pleased when a year later – following the breakup
with Tal – I stopped going.

Tal was the one who brought me to the Emin in the first place.
Although I'd made many other friends there, they all knew me as
half of a couple, as Tal's girlfriend – for Tal was a committed and
respected member of this group. I later heard he became a healer.
It didn't feel right to continue hanging around with the same
crowd, and so, I left the Emin.

I had other, more earthly things to move on to – like my final
exams at high school. I dedicated time to preparation and didn't
do too bad on these exams. Also, the mandatory military service,
which every young Israeli is expected to go through, was
looming, and I wanted to make the most out of life before

donning khaki uniform for two years. I did my best to enjoy life during that year, in that carefree and whole way that only a seventeen-year-old is capable of.

By the time I turned eighteen, Tal was not in my life anymore. As I grew up in Israel, I found myself in a place where most young Israelis find themselves at that age: the military. One thing about the Israeli military, or about any military in the world for that matter, is that it is a man's world. Yes, there are some high-ranking female officers in the Israeli military, and in other armies around the world. But mostly, it is ruled by testosterone-infused generals who are concerned with strategy – and with their own promotions. Needless to say, it is not the best place for aura-gazing.

So for a couple of years I put these things out of my mind and focused on all aspects of military life. My work was interesting – I was a liaison officer between the Israeli Ground Forces Command and other Ground Forces in foreign armies. Information exchanges and requests, combined drills and visiting officials left me little time for socializing during the week, so over the weekends, when I went home, I made sure I was not missing out. And the life of an eighteen-year-old can get very hectic, especially since I also had an exciting new person who arrived in my life in my nineteenth year: my baby brother Michael.

Michael was born when I was in officers' training, and just before the start of a long weekend during which I was supposed to be on duty. A phone call from Ramy informed my superiors that my mother was on her way to hospital to give birth to my baby brother, nearly nineteen years after she gave birth to me. My superiors thought it was a big enough event to let me out for the weekend, and so as soon as I got the exciting news, I hopped on a bus heading for Jerusalem. I got to the hospital just in time to see the little baby, minutes after he was born. I fell in love immediately.

Initially Michael's cot was in our parents' bedroom, and later it moved to a little enclosed terrace – for we lived in a small flat. When I was on leave from the military I'd push his pram around the streets of our town, and amazed acquaintances who had not seen me for a while would often question me with a slightly puzzled look: Is he yours?

"No," I'd answer proudly. "This is my little brother, Michael."

"Ah," they'd sigh. "What a cute baby."

I had no plans of becoming a mother at nineteen, for I had many things I wanted to do with my life – which became more and more hectic, with little or no time for spirituality. My Emin days were nearly forgotten, and the Tal-days were a distant memory, for by then I had a new boyfriend – someone who is still a dear friend twenty years later.

Not many nineteen-year-olds have time to be spiritual, and if they do, it is usually because something unusual had happened to them, or they feel a higher calling. As for me, nothing truly unusual happened in my life, and if I did have a higher calling, well, I didn't hear it. The latter might possibly be because I was too busy listening to loud music, dancing in nightclubs and going on jeep trips in the Negev Desert with people who I thought were cool. Actually, even in hindsight, they were.

My thirty months of compulsory military service, and my early twenties, passed by like a flowing river, turbulent at times but mostly heading in the right direction. However, there was one thing that always lingered in the back of my mind, and perhaps it is not so strange or unusual, for many young people crave travel and distant lands. But my own obsession, like many people before me, was with Africa.

Seven

the road to Africa

From about the age of ten, possibly earlier, I was fascinated with the African continent and read any book I could get my hands on which was set in this land of magic and tragedy. I even wrote one of my two final papers at University about the Civil War in Angola. Why Angola? Why Africa? I had no idea, and it would take me some twenty years to come up with an answer. But in the meantime, I was satisfied with reading books such as *The Poisonwood Bible*, *The Catastrophist* and *Out of Africa* – again and again.

Something about this continent fascinated me, and the more I read about it, the more I was convinced that I must visit it one day. And this day could not come soon enough.

I managed to get a student job – for I needed to pay my university fees – as a flight attendant with El Al, the Israeli airlines. Other than dealing with sometimes difficult passengers and waking up in the middle of the night to work on flights to Bucharest, Prague or one of my favorites – the 7 am flight to New York, this job was every student's dream. Visiting new places and meeting interesting people – even if what remained after paying the rent for the Tel Aviv flat, which I shared with a roommate, and the tuition at university was close to nothing – it was the experiences that mattered.

While fellow students waited tables at local restaurants, served drinks at crowded bars or cleaned other people's homes to make ends meet, I – while still serving meals and drinks and working crazy hours – was able to wear an elegant uniform and see the world. I felt as if I was truly one of the lucky ones.

I even got free standby tickets for flights once a year. So when I was on a rebound from a failed relationship with another boyfriend, at the age of twenty-two, I took two weeks off work and used a standby ticket to catch a flight to South Africa – for there is nothing like travel to heal a broken heart.

This was 1994, a few short months after Nelson Mandela was elected president of South Africa. When the plane touched down at Johannesburg International Airport I could hardly contain the feeling of exhilaration. Something about the air I breathed in as I disembarked from the plane was excitingly new, but strangely familiar, at the same time. The breaking dawn, the sounds, the voices and the faces of the people around me made me feel as if this was a déjà vu. It was the first time in my life that I was visiting the African continent, yet I felt at home right away.

I spent two weeks backpacking around South Africa, and this was one of the most memorable times in my life. I started the trip with a travel partner, someone I met through some contacts before I left home, and when I realized that this partner was not someone I enjoyed spending my days with, I found another traveling companion. This was an Australian young man, in his early thirties (which at the time seemed quite old) who was not only entertaining and good company, but also adventurous and exciting. Together we went diving with sharks, hitchhiked and stayed with families who invited us to spend the night or the weekend. I felt alive every single moment of that journey.

During those years of my early twenties, it was all about taking in life, experiencing and exploring the limits – my limits.

I suppose that limits come in all sorts and forms.

A few months after the South Africa trip, I met another young man. He was tall and handsome – and was not the adventurous type. It seemed that all he wanted was stability – which I did not think was right for me at the time – but despite that fact, when he proposed only three months after we met, I found myself saying 'yes'.

Until this day I am not quite sure where this 'yes' came from – I suppose I thought that a white wedding and a young, handsome husband were another sort of boundary I was conquering. It was a new experience – one that many of the young women my age were looking for, longing for – and I felt unable to push it away. I had to try married life, too.

The less said about this period of my life, the better. Not that it was bad in any way – this young man was a good person and an overall 'nice guy' – but it was simply not the 'real me' – it was someone else enjoying the city life, eating out in restaurants and visiting bars, living the poster-child life of a twenty something with nothing to look forward to. But it was not enough to keep me happy.

So after a five-year stint as a flight attendant – which helped pay the bills as a student and fulfil my passion for travel around the world – and armed with a bachelor's degree in Political Sciences and International Relations, I applied for a training program with the Israeli Foreign Office – and was accepted.

I don't recall a conscious decision to focus on the here and now. I was now in my mid-twenties, a married woman, a respectable and productive member of society, and part of a well-greased political mechanism. Isn't this what most of our parents wish for us to become? Mine did, and they were happy and proud. My mother and both my fathers, my biological father, Harry, who lives in Canada, and my stepfather, Ramy, were thrilled for me.

I, too, was satisfied with my life, at least on the surface. At work, I was surrounded by interesting, intelligent people, and most of the conversations that were held in the corridors and in official meetings were of political nature. Conversations about politics can give you the somewhat errant impression that you can actually make a difference to people's lives by talking about what others should be doing. And I certainly wanted to make a difference – I didn't know how, but back then, politics seemed important.

At home, I had a doting husband, a good and kind man. Not

adventurous, not exciting, but certainly caring and loving. It should have been enough to keep me happy, but somewhere deep down I knew that it wasn't. Something was missing in my life – it was not something tangible, not something I could put my finger on or point at. Not something I could define in words. Today, I can certainly find those missing words – they were *adventure* and *exploration*.

So when adventure came knocking at my door, in the form of an offer to be posted to Luanda, Angola, effective immediately, despite my husband's strong hesitation, I said 'yes'.

Eight

can past lives really exist?

It wasn't until my brother Michael died that I was thrown into this feeling of being on the outside, looking in. I believe that in psychology they call it 'dissociation' – a twelve-letter word for an otherwise difficult-to-describe sensation. Also sometimes referred to as an 'altered state of consciousness', it was almost as if my body and my soul were separate at times. The feeling was not completely unfamiliar, as I suddenly remembered feeling it as a child, almost nightly. Coming back to it during difficult moments was comforting in a strange way.

For the entire twenty years Michael was alive, I was part of what I considered to be 'normal life'. I was married for the second time now to a wonderful man, living in Europe, and had two young boys.

I had had my share of adventure, and finally felt ready to settle down in a small village near the French-Swiss border, a place that – not unlike Africa – felt like home from the moment I set foot in it. The language was not easy to learn, but it had a charming, melodic and romantic sound to it. It was even somewhat familiar, as I always loved listening to French music and watching French films. Since I was a child, I enjoyed learning languages and I happily delved into my studies of French and into the magic of motherhood and of writing.

I'd made many friends and I now had a husband who was as adventurous as I was, and two children who were often a challenge but always a gift.

Then, when Michael died, something in me changed, or rather, regressed to the way I used to be as a child and as a young woman. Somehow, the spiritual side of me completely took over the 'down to earth' side, and as I had more and more experiences of communicating with the world beyond ours, I also felt more and more detached from people around me, even from my very own body.

I started having out of body experiences again. Now I knew that this phenomenon had a name and I also knew that it was somehow connected to the state of grief and shock I was in following my brother's death. Nonetheless, I was surprised how the people around me reacted to these changes in me.

It is never easy being near someone who has experienced the sudden death of a loved one – it is almost as if it is a disease that people are afraid to catch. Many don't know how to approach mourning – it is awkward, no doubt. The alienation I felt from many whom I considered close friends made me go even further into the world of spirits – a world that felt welcoming, familiar and more understanding of what I was experiencing than the humans that physically surrounded me. With a few exceptions, whenever I was with people I used to think of as close friends in the past, I felt alone and misunderstood. Whenever I meditated, I felt warmth and comfort. And so, as my ties with the world beyond deepened, my ties with the physical world loosened and I started looking at life and death in a new way. And, I was keener than ever to explore things further. It was Michael's death that pushed me onto this path. Without it, I would have probably still be wandering around life, too busy for spirituality.

People's fear of death in Western society astounds me today even more than it did back then. For death is the only certain thing in life, and despite this cliché being an absolute truth, with only the timing varying from one person to another, we never seem to be prepared for it. It is regarded as an end, as final and as negative, not as the metamorphosis it might be – the release of a spirit from physical to energy form, not unlike a caterpillar turning into a butterfly and experiencing newfound freedom from the limitation of eternal crawling in search of sustenance.

In the months following Michael's death, I found it easier to close my eyes and communicate with ghosts than to face the uncomfortable stares of people in town. Once or twice I was stopped on the street by well-meaning acquaintances, expressing their condolences, and although their intention was kind, I felt my eyes fill with tears. In the spirit world, no one made me cry. There was just this feeling of total comfort, of warmth, of *a knowing* that made it all better.

That was when I first heard of Tatjana, a hypnotherapist specializing in past life regression. Why past lives? The real answer is, I don't know. I suppose it was the right time and place to explore a new direction, and with the – justified or unjustified – feeling that I had no real support from close friends, I desperately needed something to cling on to.

It took a few weeks before I found the courage to contact her and book an appointment. She said it would be good to come with some kind of idea of what I wanted to work on, to have something that she called 'an entry point', rather than just come without anything specific.

"It would be like embarking on a trip without a destination," she said. "Sure, you'll get somewhere, but not necessarily where you were hoping to go."

I liked Tatjana's down-to-earth attitude, and I didn't have to think long and hard before I knew what I wanted to work on: that feeling of alienation, the disconnectedness I often felt in many group situations. That would be my entry point.

As the day of my appointment approached, I felt my nervousness increasing. What would it be like? Would I discover something that would help me understand more about who I was and what I was all about? I even entertained the idea of cancelling the appointment. Perhaps I wasn't ready to explore something so extreme. But then I dismissed the thought. What's the worst that could happen? Perhaps I would get 'stuck' in a past life? But I wasn't even sure I believed in past lives, so how could I get stuck in something that didn't exist?

Finally, the day and time came, and I drove to the meeting. Tatjana's practice was located in the Pâquis of Geneva, a small artsy neighborhood full of little shops, bars and restaurants. I felt nervous as I parked my car, thinking it is my last opportunity to cancel.

Was I really ready for something like this? Perhaps I sensed that this was one meeting that would take my life in a new direction. I decided to give it a go.

I didn't know what to expect when the door opened, but I was surprised to see a woman in her late thirties or early forties – for some reason I assumed she would be older. Tatjana was calm, her dark eyes serious and her office spacious and airy. I looked around and saw two comfortable armchairs, a couple of bookcases, a desk, a therapy bed. She asked me to sit on one of the chairs.

"What brought you here?" she asked, and I told her of my brother's death, of my feeling of disconnectedness from people who were previously close friends and of my embarkation on a spiritual journey. She wrote it all down.

"Is there a place in the world you feel particularly drawn to?" she continued.

I did not have to hesitate, for I immediately knew the answer. It was Africa.

After this short interview, she asked me to lie on the bed and she covered me with a blanket.

"Under hypnosis," she explained, "your body temperature goes down, so it is best to keep you warm."

As I took a few deep and slow breaths and listened to Tatjana's soft voice, I started to relax. I was familiar with relaxation and meditation techniques, as I had been practicing yoga for quite a few years. This did not feel very different from a state of deep relaxation. I concentrated on my own breathing, but could still hear the raindrops tapping on the window, which calmed me even further. I did not feel afraid, or worried. It felt good to lie there and put all my worries aside for a short while.

Now I was heading towards Africa in my mind's eye, as Tatjana described a rotating globe, which I could see in my imagination. Then we stopped on the map of Africa and zoomed in. Tatjana instructed me to imagine myself going into the continent and landing onto a spot on the map. It didn't matter what country it was in, or if I even knew the name of the country.

"Just pick a spot," she said. Once I have, she asked me to take a few moments, and look around me. Then I was to describe what I saw.

An important step in hypnosis is to let your mind run free, not to put limits on it or restrain it with the voice of reason. The conscious mind doesn't always want to lose control, and often has its own agenda. We are so used to making mental lists and thinking about what we've got to do later that hour, day, week…that it is sometimes difficult to just let go and allow ourselves to delve into the depths of our minds.

So there I was, somewhere in Africa, emerging out of the mist that surrounded me like a large, fluffy cotton-ball.

"Look down at your feet," said Tatjana. "Now tell me what you can see."

After a brief hesitation, I looked down, and in my mind's eye I could indeed see a pair of feet. On the left foot I noticed something that resembled a ring. The feet looked dusty, and quite wide. A man's feet.

It was hard to be certain that I wasn't making the entire thing up – but I told Tatjana what I saw. Suspending disbelief is key in hypnosis – today I know this.

She kept guiding me through my journey, asking questions: What was I wearing? What did the place I was at look like? What else did I notice?

I told her everything I could think of, and allowed myself to say whatever came to my mind without stopping to think whether this could be a real memory, or perhaps just an imagined story.

Later I learned to recognize this process as 'grounding in the past life body' – helping the hypnotized person notice details about his or her past life body, details that can become significant later but that probably would go unnoticed otherwise. For who in the world looks at their feet and describes them in such detail without being asked specifically to do so?

When asked, I was able to notice details: feet, and a body with chocolate-color skin and not much more – only something that resembled a loincloth or a rag loosely wrapped about the middle.

"Are you a woman or a man?" asked Tatjana, and I could say with quite a bit of certainty that it was a man's body. As she led me into that experience, I became aware of more and more details around me, but there was one thing I found difficult to connect to – feelings. Even when Tatjana asked me what I was feeling in that body, or what I was feeling in a particular situation, I could experience a very vague sense of emotion but none of the strong feelings one associates with life, or with death. It was almost as if I was watching a movie, with myself in the lead role.

I could tell I was living at the edge of a village, and I was some kind of medicine man, or healer. I didn't have a family, and people would come to me only when they needed something – advice, a cure, a blessing or a curse. It was quite a lonely existence, and one that I felt very comfortable with. The trees, the rich smell of the red earth and the frugal existence – that was all I needed to feel content in the situation I was experiencing so vividly.

Before bringing me back to the here and now, Tatjana took me down a path in the forest, and asked whether I could see a spirit guide, or get a message that is relevant to my life.

I struggled at first, for I didn't know if I even believed in spirit guides. My conscious mind kicked in and asked, *Spirit Guide? What's that? Am I looking for a wise old man? Perhaps for an angelic being?*

This did not make much sense to me, and I could not see, or even imagine, another person on the forest path. Neither could I see a being of light or a man with a long white beard. Nada. I told Tatjana that I could not see a thing.

"That's all right," said Tatjana. "Just keep walking."

I kept walking down the forest path, and enjoyed the shadow of the trees and the sound of the birds. And then, in my mind's eye, I could see something fluttering behind me, and I turned to see what it was.

It was a beautiful, huge dragonfly.

"I can't see a spirit guide," I said to Tatjana. "All I can see is a dragonfly."

"Ask it if it has a message for you, or a gift," she instructed, and I did.

I then felt a cape being wrapped around my shoulders, and when I looked at it I could see its beautiful colors – purple and blue with hues of dark pink. Somehow, I knew this cape was for protection. And that I should imagine wrapping it around me every time I felt I needed it.

When I came out of the hypnotic trance I felt as if I was still floating in a dream. Some kind of deep realization, a sudden *knowing* of why I'd often felt distant when in big groups, washed over me in a warm wave of comprehension. The feeling I had during the regression, of being on my own, living in solitude and connecting with spirits more than with living people, was familiar and comforting. It did not feel strange or uncomfortable, and I wondered if it had somehow accompanied me into this life.

"Why didn't I see a spirit guide?" I asked Tatjana. "Maybe I don't even have one."

"Everyone has spirit guides," she said. "They are always there for us, but they manifest themselves in such a way they know we can accept them."

"So my spirit guide is a dragonfly?" I asked, slightly baffled.

She just smiled and shrugged.

I thanked her and left her practice feeling a little dizzy, but elated. The people I passed on the street somehow looked more real, the colors around me more vivid. I noticed small details that I did not see before – the smoke coming out from the exhaust pipe of the bus that passed on the street; a lady wrapping herself tightly in her deep-blue coat, for a chilly wind had started blowing. I felt very alive, very connected to myself, my body and the street I was walking on, as if until now I had been looking at life through some kind of smoke screen – and this screen had suddenly been lifted.

The most surprising thing was that following this regression, I hardly ever experienced the feeling of alienation again, and every time I got close to feeling it, I immediately remembered where it came from – perhaps from a past life as a healer in Africa, as a lonely man who did not have family or friends and was socially awkward. Most important, the question of why I used to feel disconnected did not bother me anymore like it had in the past. The understanding of the roots of the inconvenience I had experienced all my life, even if there was the possibility that these roots were imaginary, changed the way I looked at life as a whole.

Nine

delving in deeper

I couldn't believe my luck. I managed to book a ticket for Brian Weiss' November workshop in London just before they were all sold out.

I took the very early morning flight from Geneva, as the event began at nine. I had arranged to meet my friend Aneta, whom I met during my Regression Therapy training, a few moments before the start of the event.

When I got there a long queue already snaked at the entrance, and I spotted Aneta and waved to her. I knew she'd save me a seat.

Dr. Weiss is a successful American psychiatrist who, by his own account, had stumbled onto past life regression by chance – when he treated one of his patients with normal hypnosis. In his first book, titled *Many Lives, Many Masters,* he tells the tale of how this patient, whom he calls Catherine, had spontaneously regressed into what seemed to be a past life. Then, on subsequent sessions, he had purposefully regressed her into many other lives – and she told him of the most amazing experiences, full of details which were too specific to have been made up and of messages from the beyond.

Dr. Weiss had lost a son many years before, only a few days after this baby was born. No one outside his immediate family knew of this tragic occurrence. No one, except Catherine that is, who under hypnosis even told him why this happened and how the death of his newborn son was supposed to put him on a specific path in life.

He was a mainstream psychiatrist back then, not an especially spiritual person, and he treated these sessions with initial suspicion. However, as he became convinced that such impossible events were indeed possible, he then spent most of his life researching the phenomena of past life regression. He became one of the pioneers in this field and wrote several books on this topic – most of them becoming instant best sellers.

I booked a place for his workshop, thinking that it might help advance my own search for answers, and my research about what is true and what is fantasy. I was now convinced that there was indeed something beyond our everyday life – but what was that 'something'?

I'd read a couple of Dr. Weiss' books several years back and was not sure what to think of them. The fact that he himself was initially skeptical about spiritual matters made his story more credible to me. He headed some of the most respectable departments and programs in the US, until this one patient changed his life. *He wasn't just another airy-fairy guru*, I thought to myself. *Maybe I would find some answers if I went to listen to him speak.*

Now, more than two decades after he wrote his first book and thousands of patients later, Dr. Brian Weiss stood on a stage in front of a packed hall of several hundred people, and talked about his experiences with past life regression. His voice was confident and reassuring, his face that of a man who had seen a few things in his life – which by then spanned some seven decades. He transported everyone present into a parallel reality.

Most of the things he talked about were not new to me, as by now I had read several more of his books as preparation for this workshop, as well as quite a few other ones dealing with hypnosis, past life regression, and reincarnation.

"Close your eyes," Dr. Weiss' soft voice echoed across the vast hall as he led us into group hypnosis, through relaxation and visualization – two very powerful tools.

At this point, having woken up at 4 am to catch the flight from Geneva and having rushed through the morning traffic in bustling London, I needed to relax. The only problem was that I relaxed so deeply that I simply fell asleep.

The next thing I remembered was Dr. Weiss counting back from ten to one, and me waking up – feeling refreshed and happy. No memories of a past life, no memories of anything. Just a very relaxed disposition and a warm and pleasant feeling, as if I had rested for hours.

This whole regression exercise did not take more than twenty minutes, but when under hypnosis, time has a very different pace – almost as if it becomes elastic. Minutes can feel like days, and days can feel like minutes.

I looked at the faces of people around me and could tell from their expressions that for many of them, this was a life-changing experience.

"What did I miss?" I asked Aneta, and she smiled at me.

"Not much," she said.

One of the things I like about Aneta is that she is very down to earth. I like to think of myself as down to earth as well – a spiritual kind of down-to-earth person.

Spirituality and gullibility are often confused, for so many people have been taken advantage of by self-appointed gurus and greedy charlatans. But both Aneta and I wanted to experience things for ourselves before we decided whether they were real or not. Which was exactly why we were sitting there, staring at each other and smiling.

"He did a normal group hypnosis session," whispered Aneta, "but I didn't feel anything."

"Hmm…" I whispered back. "I wonder what the others experienced."

The silence that enrobed the hundreds of people sitting together, dreamy-eyed, was powerful and poignant. I felt as if something important had just happened – and I had totally missed it by falling asleep.

Then Dr. Weiss asked people from the audience to share some

of their experiences, and hesitantly, a few hands were raised.

A woman in her late fifties was the first to speak.

"I cannot even begin to tell you how I feel," she said. Her voice was strained, emotional.

"For many years I've had problems with my family, my brothers and sisters. We have a family house..." she started, before breaking down in tears.

She went on to tell a lengthy and painful family tale, and I could not stop myself from thinking how strange it must feel for this woman to tell her personal story in front of so many strangers. It reminded me a little of the Oprah Winfrey television show I had watched a few times while visiting the United States – and wondered why would these people share their deepest thoughts and feelings with strangers. But then, I thought, perhaps it makes them feel better – so who am I to judge? It is possible that sharing things with strangers whom you'll never see again is easier than sharing them with those closest to you.

When booking this workshop, even if subconsciously, I was hoping to somehow connect to Michael and try and understand what has happened to him – and to me since he died. Why had I suddenly taken this path?

True, I was a pretty spiritual teenager, but then life took me in another direction. I'd become a skeptic and a very grounded person.

True, I'd lost my beloved brother. But plenty of people lose loved ones and don't go off on a quest of the nature of the afterlife – they simply bury themselves in work, or in other relationships, or in alcohol. So why was I suddenly going from one spiritual workshop to another, as if a back wind was pushing me in that direction?

I did not get the answer to that question at Brian Weiss' workshop, but I did get something else, which was useful: I saw the power of hypnosis and its healing benefits to the masses. Of course, not everyone would go and spend a day at a past life regression workshop. But those who did, seemed to come out calmer, more serene. These are not the people who'd then go out and rob a bank or steal a car. The thought that there is something beyond this world, and that you might be held accountable for your actions in this life, makes people feel differently about their entire lives. It makes them better human beings. The only question that remained with me was – is it really possible, or is it just wishful thinking?

I hugged Aneta as we parted that evening, happy to have spent the day exploring something that was so important to me, with a friend that was so like-minded.

Ten

one cold winter

I cannot move my legs. It feels as if they are trapped. Then I feel terribly cold; I start shivering.

"Where are you?" asks Katherine.

"I think…I think I am in some kind of cave, a sheltered place in the mountains," I answer.

In fact, I am stretched on a bed, covered with two blankets. But in my mind, I am elsewhere.

"Are you a man or a woman?" asks Katherine.

"A woman, a young woman…" I whisper.

It is often difficult to explain things clearly during a past life regression session. The images come quickly, and are not always in focus. Sometimes it is just a feeling of 'knowing' something, identifying a detail or a piece of information. People can experience something that feels like flashes of memories from the distant past. Others can even hear or 'feel' words, even entire phrases.

I shiver again, feeling overwhelmed by the cold.

"What are you wearing?" asks Katherine.

She is trying to help anchor me in that body. In a hypnotic state, it is easier to notice things when someone asks about them. By noticing specific details, such as clothing, the experience feels more real, less detached.

I focus on the images behind my eyelids. At first, they are not easy to identify, I have to let them float without imposing a meaning on them. Just let them come up. And then I know, as if someone has suddenly turned on the light.

"I am wearing a winter coat," I say. "And winter boots. But I am cold, so cold."

"Tell me about your thoughts," says Katherine. I hesitate.

"I hope someone will find me," I say. I feel lost. It feels as if I've been wondering around for a long time before finding this sheltered place.

"Tell me more," instructs Katherine, and I try to focus on the blurry images. And then I know.

"I live somewhere near the mountains – perhaps even near the Jura mountain range, where I live today," I start.

My present day consciousness is always there; I am never out of touch. I am present, yet I allow myself to speak of the images and insights I have, without trying to logically analyze them.

"I was upset with my parents, and went off wandering on my own. Now I am lost, I don't know what to do," I continue. I feel sad, worried.

"Tell me about your family," asks Katherine. The answers now come quickly. I just know them.

"I have a younger brother. They treat him like the prince of the family. They never ask him to do any work around the house."

"How do you feel about that?" she asks.

"I feel that my parents are treating me unfairly."

Then the rest of the story unfolds without effort.

I am a curious and intelligent young woman. I want to study, like my brother does. But I am expected to be the docile, hard-working daughter of a family living in a rural village. As a young woman of strong character, this makes me feel frustrated, and I rebel.

One morning, feeling particularly frustrated, I head off into the mountains, on my own. It is late autumn, early winder. The mountaintops are white, but the sun is out.

I dress in warm clothes, wearing my winter coat and leather boots. I put some nuts and a crust of bread in my pocket. I am determined to make a point and get my parents to understand that I, too, have the right to some time for myself and a choice of what I want to do with it. My determination makes me feel brave. I am proud of myself for taking a stand.

Until I get lost.

I am completely living, or perhaps re-living, this experience. As Katherine guides me through the story by asking questions, making me pay attention to details, it becomes clearer and clearer that I am in deep trouble.

It is late in the day. The temperatures drop quickly. I am on my own, with no one who knows where I went or where to go looking for me. This doesn't feel like such a good plan anymore.

"What happens next?" asks Katherine, encouraging me to advance along the storyline of that past life. The details are vivid and the emotions strong. While going through them, I never stop or doubt that it is indeed a past life.

I describe in detail how I feel. I think that if I don't get out of the shelter and try to find my way back home I will surely die there, and no one will find my frozen body until many months later, when winter ends and the snow melts.

"I have to get out of here," I mumble. "I have to find a way out of the mess I've gotten myself into. I don't want to die."

I move my stiff legs, trying to get the feeling back into them so I can walk again, and I step out of the shelter.

Earlier that day I walked up the mountain in the sun and trod on soft, freshly fallen snow. Now, with the plummeting temperatures, the powdery snow turns into a layer of merciless and slippery ice.

I feel cold, I feel afraid, but I must find a way back to my house, where my parents and brother are surely waiting, sick with worry. I now realize how foolish I've been. Yes, they expect a lot of me. Yes, I would like more freedom. But is this worth dying for?

I continue walking, my feet aching and my spirit very nearly broken.

"What happens next?" asks Katherine.

The details flood in.

"I see a light in the distance," I say, my voice barely audible. "I see a flickering light."

"A light? Where is it coming from?"

I try to see. It is not coming from a house, for it is moving towards me.

"I don't know," I say softly. "Maybe it's someone holding a lantern."

I call towards the light.

"Hello, hello…anyone there?"

The silence is overpowering, but I am encouraged to see that the light is a little brighter than it was before. And then it stops. I start weeping, and the light starts moving towards me again.

As the light gets closer, I see a man wearing strange looking leather-bound snowshoes. There's a dog at his feet, a large and very hairy mutt.

The man holds his lantern in front of him, trying to see the way. The lantern is made of steel, and looks heavy, but the light it gives is heavenly – warm and promising.

The dog reaches me first and barks. It is a friendly dog, wagging its tail at me enthusiastically. I can now see it is a scruffy-looking hybrid pup, its fur all tangled up and messy, but its eyes shining and its breath warm, coming up in a mist towards my nearly frozen face. I let myself collapse, and the dog licks my cold cheek.

As the man approaches, I get a glimpse of his face and my first thought is that he doesn't look very different from the mutt. He is tall, his head and half his face are covered by a fur hat from which his hair sticks out in an uncombed mess. He is perfectly equipped for this cold weather and as he kneels down and talks to me I notice that he smells warm and wonderful, like leather and earth and fresh air all combined.

I can still recall that smell as I write these lines, even if it is indeed a smell from over a century ago.

"What happens next?" asks Katherine.

The man navigates down the mountain in the dark, supporting me all the way back to my village, back to my home. The layer of ice is getting thinner and the temperatures rise as we descend. I then realize that I was not that far from home really. I just got disorientated, distracted by my self-pity and my anger at my family.

By the time the man delivers me to my parents the moon hangs over us like a loyal chaperon, and my parents are grateful and invite him in for a drink. After I warm up by the fire, a blanket over my shoulders and another over my knees, I look at the man's face for the first time since he has taken off his furry hat. It is on the ground, by my feet, where my mother has put it to dry by the fire.

He is in his mid or late twenties, his eyes dark and tender, his cheekbones high. He acts awkward at first, but then he starts joking with my parents and makes them laugh, and I am the one suddenly feeling awkward. I find myself unable to take my eyes off his face. I think that it is not a strikingly handsome face, but it is a wonderful face nonetheless. The face of a guardian angel.

The young man stays with us for a short while, his dog sitting silently at my feet, enjoying the heat from the fireplace. I stroke his head, and he puts his chin on my knees, asking for more.

The man refuses an invitation from my parents to stay for dinner, and heads off to his own home, a good hour's walk in the dark. We do not exchange a word that whole time, but he tells my parents that he teaches the children of a well-off family in town. He likes his job. He likes teaching and he likes the children. No, he doesn't have any of his own. No, he isn't married.

He comes to visit several times over the coming weeks, usually on Sunday afternoons, and sits with us for tea and apple pie. Three months or so later, a marriage proposal arrives. I am at once delighted and perplexed.

I am a pretty young woman, from a farming family that is not at all well off but has hopes of marrying off their daughter to a wealthy man. A teacher with a modest income and a disheveled appearance is not exactly what my parents have in mind, even if he had saved my life.

"I don't know," says my mother as she braids my hair. "He is obviously a good man, but what kind of a life are you going to have with him?"

As for me, what did I know? I was very much influenced by my parents' opinion and by that of neighbors and relatives. Everyone concludes that although this young man is a kind-hearted and intel-

ligent person, I should aim for more.

And this 'better prospect' arrives a short time later, when the son of a well off family from the nearby town starts courting me. He is handsome and has a promising future as a merchant, for his father owns a shop, and although I never feel as safe and comfortable with him as I do with the teacher, who by then has become a part of my life, I let myself be convinced by my family that it is a much better idea to marry the merchant than the kind-hearted schoolteacher. And so, I do.

Katherine listened to my story with what she later told me was pure fascination, as tears started rolling down my cheeks. The tale was extremely detailed and clear, and I was able to recover these details later when I listened to the recording of the session. It was nearly two hours long, but felt like minutes.

The end of that life was not a happy one. My marriage was not satisfying and I kept seeing the schoolteacher around town, but we did not exchange another word. He never married, and when he died many years later, I cried inconsolably at his funeral, as I had no doubt that it was him whom I should have spent my life with; I should have gotten over the barrier of appearances and social status and listened to my own heart. Instead, I spent over forty years with a husband that I did not love, and despite the fact he gave me two children, I was never as happy as I hoped I'd be.

Regrets are terrible things, especially when they are addressed at something you did a century or two ago. At the end of that life I felt that I had badly disappointed someone, as well as myself, and I betrayed his faith in me. He saved my life and offered me love, friendship and kindness, and I gave him nothing in return. Warm tears ran down my cheeks at the end of that regression session, as the tender feelings towards this wonderful man and the regret for not spending that life with him and for disappointing him so badly came rushing into my now-awake consciousness. Katherine stuffed a tissue into my hand. I clutched the wet piece of paper and sobbed.

Eleven

messages from beyond

Have you ever wondered how a psychic gets the messages they do, and how they know if these messages are real? I have. I've always wondered how, in the clutter of information that inhabits our brain, with all the stimulation that attacks our senses daily, there is a possibility to create this safe space for messages that come from outside this world, and how do we know these are true messages and not a creation of our imagination.

I should start by confessing that I've always gotten what I thought might be messages from somewhere, but I haven't always listened to them. On the numerous occasions I've let these messages through, I've more often than not been surprised by how much sense they've made, and how well they've corresponded to what was happening in my life at the time. I used to say I've got good intuition – and this is how many people interpret these feelings they get about different things. Nothing more than intuition.

Then, after Michael died, I started getting more and more messages. And the more messages I accepted, the more I seemed to be getting. It was like opening the floodgates to a stream of information that was always there, but once I had actually let it in, it almost never stopped. By the time I was in the middle of my Regression course, I started getting a few messages for other people. I asked myself these questions: What do I do with these messages? How do I know if they're even real?

While at the Regression course I experienced something that made me cautious about delivering messages without filtering them first.

It was the second evening of the first course, and we were all invited to gather in the main room to watch a channeling session.

It was not officially part of the course, as evenings are free for those who wish to do other things – but we were all there, eager to watch Janet channel.

Janet, the teaching assistant, is a pleasant-looking woman in her late thirties, who formerly worked in London. Now she was a full-time hypnotherapist – and channel. She has a particular talent for moving earth-bound spirits 'on to the light' – even the most reluctant ones. Or so I'd been told.

So of course I was there, filled with curiosity and a good amount of skepticism, waiting to watch the first channeling session in my life. I'd heard and read before there were people who channeled spirits. They let the spirits use their bodies and vocal cords to speak through them and convey messages. I did not believe this was real – but of course, to watch it happening before my very eyes would be a fascinating adventure and would help me learn more about mediums and mediumship.

In my short conversation with Janet earlier that afternoon, I told her of my own experience with the lonely energy that kept setting off the fire alarm.

"Where were you?" I asked Janet. "And do you think this could be for real or was it all just fantasy?"

Janet then told me of her parallel experience and exchange with the spirit of this deceased, lonely woman.

Now Janet sat in front of us in a comfortable armchair.

"Would anyone else like to try to channel with me?" she asked. "My guide says there are many spirits who would like to connect with us."

I hesitated for a brief second. If channeling wasn't real anyway, as I believed at the time, why not play along and have some fun? But then, something stopped me – perhaps it was my common sense – and I decided to satisfy my curiosity by watching.

Two young women volunteered – Heather and Laura – and sat

next to Janet. Janet closed her eyes and took a deep breath. A few silent moments later, her eyelids started fluttering and her face took on a peculiar expression. Her mouth contracted into what looked like a forced smile, and slowly, she started talking in a high-pitched voice – quite different from her own, natural one.

Of course, if she really wanted to fake this, she could, I thought to myself.

"Hello everyone," she said. "It is nice to see so many of you here today. My name is Zachariah."

As she spoke these words, her hands started shaking slightly and she clasped them together. Her eyelids continued fluttering.

Hazel, one of our two instructors, sat on a chair next to Janet, and was acting as the interviewer in this channeling session.

"Hello, Zachariah," she said. "It's so good to have you back with us."

"It is so good to talk with you," said Zachariah in Janet's voice.

"Would it be all right if we went around the room and people asked some questions?" proposed Hazel.

"Yes, that would be good," agreed Zachariah.

"So, who wants to go first?" asked Hazel.

Slowly, we went around the room, and each one of us in their turn asked Zachariah a question. The answers were humorous, often very general – but sometimes surprisingly accurate.

"How is my mother doing?" asked Anna, who had recently lost her mother to cancer.

"She is doing well," said Zachariah. "She is grateful to you for being there with her in her last days and supporting her."

Anna, who sat next to me, clutched my hand and started crying. Apparently, this was true. She did nurse her mother in her last days before she died. But did Janet know this before, I wondered. Perhaps she knows Anna well and knows some things about her life. After all, we are not such a big group of people.

Then it was my turn. Should I ask about Michael? What answer would I get? And how would I know if it is real?

I decided to ask something else.

"Why do I often feel uncomfortable in big groups of people?" I asked Zachariah. "I am beginning to think that I feel more comfortable in the company of spirits than of that of some people," I added.

Zachariah's answer was immediate.

"Because you are first of all a spirit, and only then human," said Janet.

It made sense, I suppose. Others asked about their life struggles and about family issues. Zachariah's answers always came promptly, without hesitation, always carrying a message of comfort that helped put things in perspective, but never offering a solution. Could Janet really do this, just off the top of her head?

The expression on her face remained strangely different from her usual one all through the channeling session, her voice high pitched and unnatural. I didn't know Janet well beforehand, but Hazel later said that the vocabulary she used during the channeling session was her own vocabulary, but used in a different way than she normally uses it.

"There are two women who would like to try and channel," said Hazel after everyone who wanted to ask a question got their turn.

"I have many beings here with me," said Zachariah. "They would love to connect with you. It has been a very long time for them."

All through Janet's channeling session, which lasted twenty or thirty minutes, Heather and Laura sat on a sofa to her right, their eyes closed and their chins resting on their collarbones. They looked as if they were sleeping, except that every now and then one of them nodded in agreement to one comment or another.

Now Zachariah suggested that 'his friends' present themselves.

"Hello, everyone, my name is Lia," said Heather in a peculiar voice. She kept nodding her head when she spoke, as if someone was moving it up and down, like a puppet on a string. Her hands, however, remained immobile on her lap.

Heather, or Lia, went on to say a few things about life in general and answered a couple of questions for people in the room. Then Laura, who sat next to Heather, presented herself as 'Shwiki'. She seemed to have some trouble expressing herself, and could not always translate what she heard in her head into meaningful words. She only said a few sentences, and then her chin dropped down onto her collarbone again.

Kia resumed talking, but after a moment or two, when Hazel asked her a question, she said, "Hazel, Heather is getting tired."

That was the sign for Zachariah to take over again, and end the channeling session.

I looked around the room, and saw a mixture of fascination and suspicion. I was not the only one doubting, thinking – is this for real?

One way or another, I was feeling sleepy and looked forward to going to bed, with the hope that the previous night's fire-alarm incident would not repeat itself. Others must have felt like me, for within minutes we were all heading to our rooms, and a few moments later, I was fast asleep.

The following morning I felt rested and ready for the day ahead, and made my way down to the dining room to have breakfast. A few people were already there, eating porridge or fruit, and chatting. I sat at a table across from Heather and Lorraine, and noticed that Heather's eyes were red, as if she'd hardly slept.

"How are things?" I asked her, scooping some jam-stained porridge from my bowl. I can't stand this thing without some jam mixed in, preferably cherry or strawberry.

Heather sighed. "I didn't sleep all night," she said.

"Why?"

"They wouldn't let me. They kept giving me messages."

I ate in silence, considering my words. Did I believe her? Yes, I suppose I did, on some level. She didn't look like one of 'those' people, who claim they hear voices talking to them, voices that no one else can hear. And yet, this is exactly what she was saying.

"What kind of messages?" I finally asked.

"I am writing a book about energies," said Heather. She went on to tell me that she'd been working for a while now on a book that deals with energies and how they can be manipulated, and she needed some answers, or clarifications, in order to be able to finish it. And this is what the voices that kept her up all night talked about – the information she needed to finish writing her book.

She didn't seem disturbed by the fact she did not sleep much a second night in a row, and was happy to have gotten those answers she was seeking, so I left it at that. The rest of the day went by very quickly, with us learning more regression techniques and practicing on each other. It wasn't until the end of the day, when we were about to go and do yet another exercise, that Heather started trembling. Her hands looked as if they were completely out of control, shaking violently.

"They are coming again," she whispered. "They are here again," she repeated, her voice turning into something between a cry and a shout. People looked at her, not knowing how to react. For most of us, it was the first time we witnessed what we'd later learn to refer to as a 'spiritual emergency'.

"They won't leave me alone," she continued, and was ushered out by one of the instructors, leaving behind several puzzled colleagues.

Later Heather told me that recently she was experiencing constant 'contact' from the spirit world, with messages coming through for different people. She even had a couple of messages for me:

"Your son, the one with the dark hair, he can see things. There are four entities in his room, and they scare him. And your other son, he thinks too much with his head, he needs to go back to his heart..."

Heather knew I had two sons, but as far as I know she'd never seen a picture of them and did not know anything about their behavior or character. And even I had to admit – her messages made sense. Adam, my now five-year-old, had been claiming for a while that 'he saw things that scare him' in his room. He did not call them 'spirits' or 'entities'. He called them monsters, and often insisted on being accompanied even when going to the toilet. I attributed this to something that five-year-olds might be going through, a passing phase. My older son, aged eight, was always extremely logical, and often refused to accept anything that did not make sense to him from an intellectual point of view; anything based on emotional intelligence. This is a problem we've been struggling with for a while. And yes, my younger son Adam, the one who 'sees things', does have dark hair. The other one doesn't.

I did not know what to do with this information at the time, and it made me very uncomfortable. Later that month, I scheduled another appointment with Tatjana, who confirmed that Adam was indeed very open energetically and that he was very sensitive to seeing and feeling energies.

"It will get easier with age," she said. "Many children are very open when they are young, and then they close up."

Tatjana did an energetic cleansing of my house, and Adam's complaints have decreased drastically. And I learned an important lesson: never give people 'messages from the other side' unless they specifically ask for them, and are ready to deal with them.

Twelve

spirit midwifery and soul-groups

The first time I'd heard of spirit midwifery I thought it was the coolest thing ever. I've always had great respect for midwifes – these women (and few men) who over the centuries had assisted laboring mothers, in bringing new life into this world. Most people focus on the processes of labor and of birth, which are very physical and for many who've experienced or attended a birth can be truly life changing. The connection to a life force – the physical life force – is such a powerful one that few can forget it once they've experienced it firsthand.

However, few people think about the soul of the baby at times like these.

According to theories found in many sources throughout various beliefs and religions, the soul of the baby joins the body at some point during the pregnancy. Some say this happens at three months of pregnancy, some say six, while others leave this timing definition more fluid. However, one fascinating aspect of some past life regression theories is the claim that it is actually the soul who chooses the body that it will reincarnate into. In books written by pioneers such as Dr. Michael Newton, patients regressed into the period before birth, or between lives, tell of a process where they are given a choice – sometimes two or three choices – of the body their soul will go into. This takes into account the life lessons they are supposed to learn in the new life. Apparently, a soul is never forced to incarnate into a specific body, but is often encouraged to do so. For example, a soul that needs to learn the lesson of dependence on others could be encouraged to reincarnate into a handicapped body. Someone who needs to learn what it feels like to be abused, perhaps because they've abused someone else in the distant past, could be encouraged to choose the body of a person that will experience abuse. Although abuse should never be tolerated in any form, the experience of learning how to deal with it, and the empowerment that might come with stopping abuse – and getting oneself out of an abusive situation – can be an important lesson.

While some might think that everyone, given the choice, would choose to reincarnate into a beautiful and perfect body, apparently, this is not the case, for a beautiful and perfect body often does not hold the lessons that need to be learned by the soul (unless this beauty and perfection is suddenly and unexpectedly lost, for example).

As fascinating as I find the theory itself, the practice is even more unusual. In what is often called LBL – or Life Between Lives – Regression, people can remember contracts and agreements they've made in the period before they were born. These agreements and contracts are made not only with oneself, but also with other souls. Which brings me to one of my favorite topics – that of soul-groups.

The theory goes that we reincarnate in soul-groups, or soul families. Back 'home', in the spirit realm, we live in communities of souls that interact and work together for many years – more than possible to count in human lives. My personal experience, when regressed by a fellow therapist to this period between lives, was life changing. Whether this memory is real or not holds little importance – for it helped me understand many things about my life and about experiences I had as a child.

I remember, as a child of four or five, not needing much the company of other children, for I'd always felt that I was never alone. Now, many children have imaginary friends and that is perfectly normal. The phenomenon is documented in many child-psychology books, and often dismissed as the child's over-active imagination.

Except, that in a regression, I remembered a very specific contract that I made with my own soul-group. Since I was one of the first ones from that group to reincarnate in this lifetime, I was reluctant to do so, even when knowing that other members of my group would join me later – much later – in life.

So then a contract, or an agreement, was made – whereby I'd be able to communicate with members of my soul-group as soon as I came down to earth, even when they remained in the spirit realms, and they would always be near me to the best of their ability, until I felt comfortable in the new body and the new life.

This memory made all the difference to the way I now looked at my childhood.

The gift that I may have brought with me, the facility of connection to other souls in my group, is perhaps the answer to many questions I've asked myself throughout my life.

Throughout life, at various significant points, I received what I at first considered as 'hunches' and now I consider as being 'guidance'. Every now and then, I'd get the feeling of recognition when meeting a new person. That person – more often than not – turned out to be significant in my life, some in more major, and some in more minor ways.

So next time you meet a stranger and feel as if you know them, perhaps you do. Often these people go on to take a significant role in your life, even if it is 'only' your third grade teacher who installed a love of learning into you. Or a stranger on a plane with whom you had a significant conversation, a conversation that helped you make up your mind about doing something in a certain way in your life. Even if you never see that person again, the mere fact that they've had such an important influence on you implies that there might be – just might be – some kind of contract between the two of you. Any attempt to try to prove this would be futile, of course – you either sense this and believe in it, or not.

However, my experience was that once you've learned the

theory and opened your mind to the mere possibility that this might be the case, your life changes in many ways.

The notion that you may not be here on your own, a solo player isolated from the rest of humanity simply because you are a separate person in a separate body, is somewhat mind-boggling. For if it is all part of a plan – a plan you yourself have helped create – then that changes everything, doesn't it? Some of the difficulties in life, events that we don't understand the reason for their occurrence, suddenly start to make sense. Or at least resonate on a deeper level, making it easier to accept and to cope with. Deaths of loved ones, accidents, difficult relationships and broken friendships – they all help teach us something. Whether we see their value as they happen or not (and we often don't), it does change the way we look at these events, especially if we can try to understand what they teach us and what we can learn from them – even when they are painful or uncomfortable.

So how do we identify someone from our soul-group? I've asked myself this question many times. And in exploring the answer, I've tried to let my intuition lead me, and came up with some amazing answers.

If you feel as if someone helps you learn things in life in a way that no other person does – it could be a family member, spouse, friend – anyone really, chances are that there's a reason for this process. Even if the learning is through a negative process – say, someone who rubs you up the wrong way, who challenges you, who makes you angry or even if it is someone who hurts you. This could still be something you need to learn on this life journey, and this person might be just the one who is helping you achieve this. Maybe, after all, you should be thanking them for the life lesson, even if you didn't enjoy it. This does not mean that an abusive situation should be tolerated. But it can be seen as an opportunity to learn a lesson of independence and courage, of getting out of what sometimes might seem as a hopeless situation in your life. In other lifetimes, perhaps you've put up with it. In other lives, perhaps you yourself were the abuser. Now, that you perhaps have a slightly wider view of events, you can make your own choices more easily.

How To 3: recognizing a member of your soul-group

Let's say you've just met someone with whom you can connect with on a deep level straight away. You just 'get' each other. This can be a friend or a lover, a stranger or someone you just spend a short time with. Their gender or appearance does not matter – there is just something familiar about them. Sometimes you develop a relationship with this person, an exchange that can last for years, and sometimes you just walk together a length of the journey.

Here are a few questions to ask yourself next time you meet someone like that:

1 Did this person showed up in a specific point in your life when you needed help or guidance?
2 Does this encounter – even if completely coincidental – feel as if 'it was meant to be'?
3 Does it feel as if you've known this person before, even though you've just met them?
4 If this is a negative experience – did it just teach you an important lesson, one that will possibly last a lifetime?
5 Can you see, in retrospect, that something this person said or did – or even an idea they gave you – changed the course of your life?
6 Did a complete stranger just show up in a difficult situation and help you in a way that was well above your expectations?

If the answer to more than half of these questions is 'yes', there is a good chance that you've met someone from your soul-group. Your friends and family members could be members of your soul-group, but they aren't necessarily. They could be other people – or souls – that share your life or a part of it, for better or for worse. You should be grateful to them for doing so, even if the journey is often difficult. It is through our most difficult experiences that we learn and grow.

Thirteen

spirit attachments

It was the first session of hypnosis I'd ever performed as a trainee therapist. My colleague and client was Paul – a tall, well-built former serviceman in his early fifties. I liked Paul from the moment we met, the previous day. I walked into the imposing mansion of Gaunts House, where the course took place, and saw a tall, white-haired man wandering around. He didn't look as if he was part of the staff, but he didn't seem lost either; he was curiously exploring his surroundings. We looked at each other, and I immediately knew he was also there for the Regression course, although several other people were walking around the grounds, some of them part of the community of volunteers who lived there, others there for different courses.

"Are you here for the Regression course?" he whispered to me. We were the only people standing in the large corridor.

"Yes, are you?" I whispered back.

"Yes. Why are you whispering?" he whispered again.

"I don't know. Why are you?" I whispered back, and then we both started laughing, and introduced ourselves, shaking hands.

It is true that something about the imposing nature of the building, something that has to do with its age and high ceilings, ancient décor and spiritual energy, causes people to talk in hushed voices, as if they don't want to disturb the peace and tranquility the place inspires. I've since learned that Paul was not only in possession of good humor and vast general knowledge, but also of an inquisitive mind, which I have come to appreciate greatly.

Now he lies in front of me, his eyes closed. Caroline, another fellow trainee, takes notes, and I am in the process of performing my first-ever hypnotic regression on another person. I use the usual script, leading him into a past life.

"Where are you?" I ask.

"I am on a ship," says Paul. "I am a young man, in my twenties, maybe younger."

"Tell me more," I say, trying to locate where exactly Paul's mind is taking him.

His voice becomes hoarse, taking on what sounds like an American accent, very different from his usual English pronunciation.

"They are taking us to fight, I don't want to go, but I'm here now, I'm here, there are bombs all around us in the water, there is fire, there is fire…"

I let Paul concentrate on the images that he sees, while his closed eyelids flutter.

"What's happening?" I then ask, once he has absorbed more of what is going on around him. He clearly is living that moment.

"I am in the water now," he whispers. "I am swimming towards land…there are people dying around me…in the water…there are bombs…in the water…"

I move him quickly out of what seems to be a stressful situation for him, and take him to the next significant event in that life.

He is walking with a group of American soldiers, single file in a jungle. When asked to describe his clothes, he gives very detailed information about his uniform and unit badge. I make a mental note to check this when I have time, and see if such a unit really existed. It is my nagging need to prove to myself that this journey that I am going through is not an imaginary one; that is it as real as it felt at those moments when another human being sheds their protective layers before my eyes, and lets me take a glimpse into their soul.

Paul goes on to describe how he walks in the mud, in the dark jungle, and his feelings of dread and misery as he finds himself in a place he does not want to be in. He keeps mentioning a dark shadow, something that he sees and that makes him feel unsettled. I do not know what that is, and do not give it much importance.

As Paul leads me deeper and deeper through his mental journey I am able to construct the picture of a seventeen-year-old American boy who volunteers to go to the army because he doesn't have anything more interesting to do back home. He is the only son of two hardworking parents who love him but do not try to decide for him what he can or can't do. I get the distinct impression that he joined the army out of boredom, perhaps mixed with the belief that he was doing something significant for his country.

He describes posters he sees everywhere, calling young men to join the army. I wonder, but don't ask – for I am not supposed to ask leading questions as a therapist – whether what he sees in his mind's eye is Vietnam, Laos or Cambodia, and if the period he describes is the early stages of the Vietnam War.

We follow the progress of Paul, or this young man, while he walks in the jungle, regretting his decision to get to that cursed place. He loses friends, brothers in arms, and finally his own life.

I am surprised by how detailed his account is, how colorful and logical. Of course, it is very possible that he's read this story in a book, or watched a film, and he is merely repeating fragments of an experience he has read about or watched. But the energy and intensity of the description are very convincing at that moment, and I just flow with it.

That is when Janet walks in. Her role is to supervise us and make sure our initial sessions go well. She was in the room before, and walked out to see another group of students while Paul's story was progressing slowly, like a birth that is not imminent but gently advancing towards a climax. And Janet takes over, and instructs the soul of the soldier that died to go to the spirit realm. While she wraps up the session, I sit next to Paul, on a wooden chair. Janet sits on his other side.

Suddenly, I feel an almost physical sensation of someone sitting on my lap. I start, for I am not sure what it is I am feeling. I can see nothing, of course.

"Do you have any questions before we bring Paul back?" asks Janet, and Caroline, who took the notes, and I look at each other.

"Yes…" I say hesitantly. "I feel as if someone just sat on my lap. What can this be?"

Janet looks at me and I see a sparkle in her eyes.

"You felt something sitting on your lap?" she asks. This does not seem to throw her off.

"Yes, I think so… It felt like something just sat on me," I say. I worry that I sound silly, for what in the world can be sitting on my lap and why?

Janet turns towards Paul, and I see in her eyes a look that makes me think that we've got just the right woman for the job.

She calls on Paul's 'higher mind', which is something I've heard of, but never seen done before. She asks him to lift a certain finger for a positive answer, and a different finger for a negative answer. Paul lifts the fingers as instructed. Later I learn more about this technique, which in the world of hypnosis is usually referred to as an ideo-motor response. This is a process where a thought or mental image brings a reflexive or automatic muscular reaction, usually outside the awareness of the hypnotized person, not unlike the reflex of instant salivation when imagining sucking on a slice of lemon or eating a delicious chocolate cake.

"Is there any energy with Paul that doesn't belong with him?" asks Janet. We all watch Paul's fingers. Slowly, hesitantly, the 'yes' finger rises.

"Is there more than one energy that doesn't belong with Paul?" asks Janet.

The 'no' finger rises.

"I am asking this energy, which doesn't belong with Paul, to go up to his throat," says Janet. "I want you to use Paul's vocal chords and talk to me."

For a few moments nothing happens. Caroline puts her pen down, and she and I stare at each other, then at Paul, then at Janet. What is going on?

Paul suddenly starts coughing and spluttering, as if something is stuck in his throat.

"Very good," says Janet calmly. "Please use Paul's vocal chords and talk to me. My name is Janet, what's your name?"

I have to remind myself to continue breathing when I notice that I've been holding my breath.

Nothing happens for a few seconds, and then Paul starts laughing. However, it is not his natural laughter, it is a low, guttural one.

"What's the matter," says Janet. "Don't you want to talk to me?"

Caroline and I continue staring at Paul. He looks as if he is asleep, but no, he is not – for he is talking to us.

"I'll talk to you, why not," he says. The voice is Paul's, but the way the words are pronounced is not.

"What's your name?" Janet repeats her question.

"Names, names…names don't matter."

"So you don't want to tell me your name…" says Janet. "That's OK. Are you aware that it is Paul's body you're in?"

Paul nods.

"When did you come into Paul's body?" asks Janet.

Paul says nothing, and she asks the same question again.

"Come on, tell me. It must be quite a long time since you've last talked to someone."

"A long time," says Paul. "A very long time."

"So when did you join Paul's body?"

"When he was in his twenties," says Paul.

"And why did you choose Paul?" asks Janet.

"Sex," says Paul without any hesitation. "I wanted to experience sex."

Janet laughs, and this gives Caroline and me permission to smile. Is she really talking to a spirit that joined Paul's body some thirty years ago, in order to experience having sex? I find this quite amusing, even touching. But...can it be real? Or is it something well-coordinated between the supervisor and the student-client, just to play a joke on the student therapist – me?

"What was your body like, when you had a body of your own?" asks Janet.

"Old, and frail, very frail..." whispers Paul. Something in the attitude of whoever was talking to us has changed, almost as if they were bringing back distant memories that caused them sadness.

I look at Janet and see that her face wears a compassionate expression, almost as if she were talking to a child.

"So you joined Paul to enjoy having a strong body?" she asks.

"Yes, a big and strong body..." whispers Paul.

"I can help you go to a place where you can have a strong body again," says Janet. "Would you like to go there?"

"No," says Paul almost immediately. "I am fine where I am."

"Don't you want a big and strong body of your own?" asks Janet. "You know, this is not your body, this is Paul's body."

"I am fine where I am," says Paul, a stubborn streak now dominant in his voice.

Janet taps gently on Paul's forehead.

"I am talking to Paul now," she says. "Paul, do you give him permission to stay in your body?"

"No..." responds Paul in a weak voice, as if speaking from the bottom of a well. "No, I want him to go."

Janet gently taps on his forehead again.

"Did you hear that?" she asks. "He doesn't give you permission to stay. You know you have to go. Don't you want to tell me your name?"

Paul shakes his head.

"I want you to imagine a light inside you," says Janet. "A small light that grows and fills you with love, can you feel it?"

Paul nods.

"And I am calling the Archangel Michael and your spirit guide to come for you and lead you to the light…"

Paul suddenly starts laughing and coughing at once.

"Michael," he says, with a bitter laughter. "Interesting choice of name."

"Is this your name?" asks Janet.

Paul nods.

Janet continues with the spirit release procedure, a procedure that in time will become both familiar and exciting every time I attend or perform one.

For in contradiction to what most of us imagine, of evil spirits exorcised with crosses and garlic in ceremonies that we might have watched in horror films, most spirits are gentle, vulnerable beings. In fact, if someone were chasing me around with a cross and garlic and threatening me, I might get a little upset too.

Earth-bound spirits used to be people, like us, but for one reason or another stayed in the earth plane instead of going to the light, where they can continue their journey. And some of them, while hanging around the earth plane, have chosen to join the energy bodies of living people, for various reasons. Michael's reason was wanting to experience sex and having a strong body, which is as valid a reason as any. Other spirits join people's energy field out of loneliness, or because they are attracted by an addiction of a person, an addiction which perhaps they shared when they had a body of their own – such as drugs or alcohol.

Spirit attachments became one of my favorite subjects to deal with as a therapist, and people who had spirit attachments released reported a newfound lightness in their lives, for these energies that did not belong with them often weighed them down and caused them to do things they did not necessarily intend to do.

A day or two after the session I asked Paul – whose judgment I completely trust – if he felt any different and if this was a real experience or something that felt made up. He said that he felt lighter on one hand, but on the other hand he felt almost like a part of him was missing. He was so used to having this other energy with him – after all, it was with him for thirty years or so – that it was somewhat hard for him to let go.

But it is good to let go of energies that don't belong with you. They can reinforce existing behavior patterns and increase addictions – for those behavior patterns, character traits and addictions are what usually draws them to a specific person in the first place. This is the only way they can get their 'fix' for they no longer have their own bodies. So one way of getting rid of energy attachments is to make a conscious decision to change existing patterns and addictions. That alone might send them away! Another way is to ask a hypnotherapist to do this for you – but you will have to make sure you don't allow new ones to take the place of the energies that were just released. As long as you have an addiction or persistent negative feelings, you will always continue being attractive to such energies roaming the earth plane in search of a welcoming home. Once you get rid of the hooks that attract earth-bound energies – for the vast majority of earth-bound energies have stayed behind because they have an issue of some sort to resolve – it is less likely that your energy field will be an attractive home to one of them. Earth-bound energies are rarely attached to healthy, happy people, because their energy field is less open than people who are addicted or generally vulnerable. Another reason to get yourself in good shape emotionally, physically and spiritually!

How To 4: get rid of spirit attachments

The best way to be rid of spirit attachments is not to get them in the first place. This means a healthy lifestyle and a positive attitude. But of course, this is not always possible.

If you suspect you might have an energy that doesn't belong with you, you can see a therapist who can cleanse your energy field, but there are several things you could do on your own:

1 Sit quietly and close your eyes. Thoughts will be coming and going – let them come and go. They don't matter.
2 Say out loud or in your mind (whichever feels better for you), "I am asking any energy that doesn't belong to me to leave."
3 Repeat stage two a few times, just to reinforce the message.
4 Imagine a portal of light and guide any energy that wants to leave towards this portal. You will be doing yourself – and the energies – a big service.

Remember, the scary movies about possessions and exorcisms are just that – stories. Treat an energy as what it is – a lost and often lonely consciousness which is on a journey, just like you are. It has taken a wrong turn, and you can help guide it home.

Fourteen

on shamans and journeying

For millennia shamans, medicine men and women dealt with diseases, curses and plain old bad luck through chants, prayers and potions. Were they all wrong, all phonies, all hallucinating humans who didn't do anything other than play around with make believe?

I wondered the same thing for many years, and did not have the time or motivation to pursue this question during the years I was busy with my everyday life – a career, a family, a hectic social life.

However, now that I've delved into the mysteries of life after death and made this initial contact with the spirit world, I found myself drawn again to the mysteries of shamanism.

As a teenager, I read most of Carlos Castaneda's books, starting with *The Teachings of Don Juan*. There were claims at the time that many of the events that were described in that book were not real – at least not what most of us would consider real. Still, they fascinated me and I wanted to know more. The opportunity presented itself a couple of decades later, when I learned to journey.

In a shamanic journey – which contrary to popular belief does not need to involve hallucinogenic mushrooms or drugs of any kind – the person who journeys is transferred to a parallel reality aided by the beating of a shamanic drum. The repetitive beat helps disconnect from the present, and whether it is an actual drum or a recording, once we disconnect from our everyday lives and allow our minds to wander, we can see wonderful things.

My first real experience with shamanic journeying was after reading an interview with Michael Harner – the founder of the Foundation for Shamanic Studies, who was also Carlos

Castaneda's anthropology professor at Berkley. In this interview ("Shamanic Healing: We Are Not Alone" – an interview of Michael Harner by Bonnie Horrigan in *Shamanism*, Spring/Summer 1997, Vol.10, No. 1) Dr. Harner explained that Shamanism is not a religion or a belief system. It is based on personal experiments conducted to heal, to get information, or do other things.

"In fact," he said, "if shamans don't get results, they will no longer be used by people in their tribe. People ask me, 'How do you know if somebody's a shaman?' I say, 'It's simple. Do they journey to other worlds? And do they perform miracles?'"

Another observation that got my attention in the article was that in our culture many consider it avant-garde if a person talks about the body-mind connection, but the fact is that the brain is connected to the rest of the body...and this has been part of many cultures for hundreds and thousands of years. What was really important about shamanism, in Dr. Harner's opinion, was that the shaman knows that we are not alone. He concluded by saying that when one human being compassionately works to relieve the suffering of another, the helping spirits are interested and become involved.

This was good enough for me. I proceeded to read several books on the subject of shamanism – by Michael Harner, Jim PathFinder Ewing, Sandra Ingerman and others. I particularly enjoyed reading the series of books by Jim PathFinder Ewing, a contemporary American shaman who also writes on a variety of related subjects in a clear, concise and unpretentious language. I enjoyed reading his books so much that I contacted him by email and asked him if he would journey for me. He agreed, and emailed me back a week later with a detailed transcript of his journey, which I found fascinating. It is printed below with his kind permission.

Daniela Journey
Thursday, June 23, 2011
3 Red Reed

Went to Bear Cave, met Bear.

Went to Sky Lodge.

Saw Daniela's teacher appear as what appeared to be Florence Nightingale (dressed in old style clothes, like a nurse, a healer); then a Nubian (Namibian?) Prince, tall, black, with tall spear, shifted back.

At her feet were honeybees flying around, and a large cauliflower.

Saw power animals: Ibis and Hawk, both Egyptian; Ibis as if depicted on a tomb wall with blocky black-and-white colors; hawk stylized like Ancient Egyptian art. Also saw a feather; was told to treat as a soul part.

Saw six-pointed star; can be useful as 'replenishment'. Worn as adornment; was told to treat it as a soul part.

Saw procession of more animals: Siberian wolf, black panther, Grizzly or Kodiak bear, a Quetzlecoatl bird (obviously a past life connection that kept shimmering, as shaman spirit); felt/saw Melchizidek energy. Saw star beings. Then, I said, "wait, I can't remember all this." It was too overwhelming.

Then, my teacher showed up. This is very rare. He rarely shows himself. He showed me how Daniela is connecting with past lives/dimensions.

He put his hand – palm out – in front of him and off to his left at 9 o'clock, and images showed up, like putting a curser on a computer over something that pops up on screen; he moved it to 3 o'clock and other power animals and images appeared; he reached out further from his body and way high at 11 o'clock and there were still more. He said these were the procession of power animals, images/feelings I was experiencing.

He said Daniela was holding all these connections/attachments. It's OK if you know where your energy is, he said, but it means when a person is doing it, that person is not all 'here', not present, but connecting elsewhere.

He said she should be made aware of it so that she can be more present and retain her energy.

I saw also that she has retained a lot of soul pieces from past lives that need to be released.

That was all.

Needed: 3 power animals: Bee, Ibis, Hawk.
Soul pieces: 1 Six pointed star, 1 feather.
Homework: Clearing/grounding/shielding exercises.
Clear out past life soul parts.
Aho.

He followed it by this personal note:

I think the notes are fairly self-explanatory.

You are "connecting" to a lot of places/times.

There's a lot of past-life energy coming forward.

This may or may not be what you wanted in regard to your inquiry, but this is what was shown to me.

I think that if you are having problems with "clearing" your house it may have to do with your connecting to other places/times via your energy body. It doesn't matter how "hard" a barrier one puts around one's living space, if you are connecting with and ushering in beings from other places energetically. I'm not saying this in any negative way, just explanation. Frankly, it was interesting to me that my teacher (who rarely, rarely shows up, stepped forward to explain this; I might have to explore it further in a future book!).

Your teacher is your spirit guide and appeared in the various guises, I think, to show that you were either connecting or in some way identifying with or leaning on information gleaned during past lives in which you were a nurse or healer of some kind and a warrior, for use or future use.

Let me say that there was too much information to be of tremendous use, since it was flooding in from past lives; the power animals/symbols/connections were useful in those times, but may not be of help today.

Regarding the "homework," you can read about grounding/ centering/shielding on our website under "articles."

I write about removing past-life soul parts in my upcoming book, "Dreams of the Reiki Shaman."

Short version: To release past-life soul parts that are holding you down energetically. You can do this by going to a quiet place away from everyone, near water, and digging a small hole, and simply blowing into it, with the intent of releasing past-life soul parts you have collected or stolen in former lifetimes; it will almost feel that you are energetically regurgitating into the hole, and then you will feel much lighter, though perhaps a little dizzy.

People have no use for past life pieces or soul parts that are not their own, but they can be accumulated; if you release them, it will help free you energetically to become "clear" or able to focus your personal energy better. It's just energetic "ballast" that you don't need.

The honeybees are there to connect with your inner spiritual resources, to help you with the "honey," golden light, that is your inner compass or guidance. It also suggests a need to connect to your feminine energy; as bees are all female (save for a few drones kept around to keep the species going).

Don't know what the cauliflower symbolizes: need to nourish?

Ibis is sacred bird of Egypt; Hawk is messenger. You might look these up and see what resonates with you about them. The feather is a symbol, I think, for your ability as a writer, which is a past-life piece coming forward.

The six-pointed star is a universal symbol for connection with Spirit; replenishment; allowing insight/ability from the universe to come forward. (You might consider meditating on the Tarot card that shows the six-pointed star; it shows beginnings, or riches of heaven being poured as water at your feet.)

If you would like for me to do the soul retrieval, it can be done long distance. Or, this is something you can do for yourself, as outlined in my books.

I hope this is helpful!

Blessings!

Jim

Jim PathFinder Ewing (Nvnehi Awatisgi)

Healing The Earth/Ourselves

www.blueskywaters.com

The question of whether these things are real or not does not have an obvious answer. I've asked myself this question many times, and following many shamanic journeys I experienced personally since (none of them as detailed and providing as much information as the one above) and many past life regressions, I've reached the conclusion that these experiences are, indeed, real. However, the reality, which they exist in, is a parallel one, not the physical, solid one that we can touch and smell and hear around us.

One theory, which is known as 'The Filter Theory' and has some support within the scientific community, is that our brain acts as a filter that limits our perception of the world. What it really means is that the brain doesn't produce consciousness, but rather acts as a filter that allows through, as Aldous Huxley – a 20th-century writer and psychedelic-drugs advocate – put it, only "a measly trickle of consciousness".

This is normally a good thing, as if indeed we are here to experience the physical world and to learn about ourselves through it, there would be no real use to have access to unlimited information. This information would only confuse us if we were not ready to deal with it and handle it. All of us can use our five physical senses to access information that can be analyzed by our conscious mind, but all of us – without exception – also have other ways of accessing information. There are other senses, perhaps better referred to as abilities, which we can develop.

Once the journey to develop these abilities has begun, and once we get a flavor of the information that can be reached by using these abilities – it is hard to go back to sensing everything only with our five limited senses.

Drugs and psychedelics are a dangerous shortcut to reaching these abilities, and while they may give us temporary access to certain information and to a feeling of euphoria – to a 'high' that can be reached by other means that are non-drug related, they take a major toll on our physical bodies, and ultimately on our minds, too.

Taking drugs takes a moment or two, while developing your psychic abilities takes a lifetime. The rewards of the first are temporary, and the consequences often devastating.

The rewards of the latter may be eternal, and have no known physical consequence – other than possibly losing a few friends, who might think you've gone strange on them.

Fear is another major factor that keeps people at distance from those who develop their psychic abilities – or from developing them themselves.

"How will I know what I might find inside myself?" one good friend asked when I told her that anyone can have psychic experiences, and that these can improve our lives. To experience these things we don't have to look outside – but inside – ourselves.

I smiled in response to my friend's question and said nothing, for it was difficult at the time to find the words to explain that whatever we find inside ourselves is perfectly OK – for in any case, we spend a lifetime with ourselves. Although we can perhaps avoid some aspects of our real selves and our real thoughts at times by keeping busy with our everyday life, there is no way of avoiding ourselves in the long term.

Fifteen

body memories

The third module of the regression course made me uncomfortable, initially. By now, I was more or less fine with past lives, spirit attachments and negative energies that don't belong with a person. But the third module dealt with body memories. I did find the theory behind the practice extremely interesting – it was the actual practice that I initially found awkward.

The theory is that when we die, our energy body carries memories. These memories usually have to do with a trauma we've had in a past life or even with the moment of death, if it was particularly traumatic or painful.

For example, a person who died when their head was chopped off in battle, will retain in their energy body the trauma of this painful death and might suffer from neck problems in their current life. Someone who was burned at the stake by the Inquisition might suffer from fire-related traumas, from an inexplicable life-long sensation of being suffocated or a feeling of helplessness (that surely comes with being burned alive).

It is terrifying to think of how many brutal forms of death mankind has developed over the millenniums of its existence. But not all deaths are man-made, of course. If you've drowned in a past life you might develop a fear of water in your current life; if you've fallen to your death from a cliff you might suffer from a fear of heights. The mind is unaware, but the energy body remembers, and when it joins a new body in reincarnation, that new body can suffer from unexplained symptoms, or even carry birthmarks and scars from a past life.

I found the work of one medical doctor particularly interesting – Dr. Ian Stevenson, former Head of the Department of Psychiatric Medicine at the University of Virginia School of

Medicine. He had researched cases of children who claimed to remember past lives, and found many birth defects and wounds corresponding to injuries sustained in the past life.

Those who want to read more about this topic can of course find Dr. Stevenson's books, but another fascinating read – which had a huge influence on me – is *Old Souls: Scientific Search for Proof of Past Lives* (Simon & Schuster, 2001) – a riveting book written by Tom Shroder, a journalist who accompanied Dr. Stevenson on some of his research voyages to Lebanon and India.

Although there is no absolute scientific proof for reincarnation, the fact is that many people and religions in the world do believe in it. This includes most Buddhists, Hindu, Druze and Jews who are familiar with the mystical teachings of the *Kabbalah*. When scratching the surface and putting fears aside, many of us can find proof of reincarnation in our everyday lives.

At this point, I no longer doubted reincarnation. But the theory of body memories still made me uncomfortable – until I started to practice it.

Before I travelled to the UK for this course, I used a technique that I was now very familiar with. I asked for some kind of inspiration – in my dreams or in any other way they can deliver it – about what I should be working on during the coming days. I often left home with some kind of idea, and if I didn't get it before I left, it always materialized while I was at the course.

This time it was a dream, something I remembered from a couple of nights before my trip. In this dream I was walking somewhere in the countryside, probably in France, probably sometime during the Second World War, as I had a notion of the fact I was dreading the Germans who were nearing our village. As I walked down a path outside the village, I noticed a pair of eyes staring at me from what seemed to be a hole in the ground – a hideout.

"Partisans!" was my first thought – in my dream. I woke up with those eyes very vividly floating before my very own. They were dark, intelligent, intriguing – a young man's eyes. As I drifted in between dream and wakefulness – which is exactly the state the mind is at when hypnotized – I tried to go back to the dream. I wanted to get a glimpse of the man's face, of who he was or might have been. I just had the strong feeling that he was someone very significant to me – that I had loved this man. But what was the meaning of this dream?

When presented with the opportunity to work on a past life, and on body memory, I went into hypnosis ready to reconnect with this dream. All I had to cling onto were the dark eyes, and the time period. Partisans. Germans. Hideout. Possibly the 1940s.

The state of hypnosis was by now almost second nature to me – not scary or awkward in any way. It becomes easy to let go and allow your mind to wander when you realize that you are actually very safe – and you are always in control.

And so when I was asked by Debbie, my colleague and hypnotist, what body sensation I had, I answered that it was of being enclosed in a small hole in the ground. Of being trapped. The nature of bodywork is such that the hypnotized person has to allow themselves to go fully into the sensation they have, and to reproduce the body position that comes with it. For me it was a need to raise my hands above my head, wanting to let myself out of the small space in which I was trapped.

Once the body position was reproduced, the information started flowing in.

I was a young woman, in rural France, and as I walked in the woods not far from my home I saw a dark pair of eyes staring at me. We looked at each other for a brief second, and then the eyes disappeared – underground, into what must have been a hideout. I did not feel brave enough to explore this further. Instead, I ran home.

Back at home, I started gathering food. A loaf of bread, some sausages, some cheese. Then, with the food hidden in a cloth, I went back to the woods, right to the place where I saw those dark eyes. I left my gift of food on the ground, and ran back home, frightened. What have I done? Who was hiding down there? Surely, such a haunting pair of eyes could not belong to an evil man – but I had no idea who this man might be.

I repeated this exercise many times in the days that followed. Every day, as I walked to the woods – careful to make sure that I was not followed – I harbored a hope in my heart that I would see the owner of the dark eyes. I can see myself even now – a girl of seventeen or eighteen, wearing a brown dress made out of rough fabric – a peasant's dress. I am carrying a bundle – sometimes bread, sometimes fruit, always something to nourish and comfort whoever was in that hideout. And always, when I reached that part of the woods, the place where I always left the food – the food from the previous day was gone.

Until one day…one day, I finally saw him. He waited for me as I approached with the bundle of food – looked me straight in the eye, and smiled. It was the sweetest, most beautiful smile I have ever seen, and it took all my fear away. I immediately fell in love with that smile – me, a simple girl from the countryside, completely charmed by a French Resistance fighter.

Startled, I dropped my gift of food on the ground, and staring into those dark eyes, walked backwards, and then ran back home, my heart thumping. The face of this young man hovered before my eyes in the days to come.

I continued walking to the woods every day, and by then my parents noticed that something was happening in my life. It could not be the daily chores of a peasant girl that made my eyes sparkle and my cheeks flushed. I then confided in my mother, who was not happy at first. Still, she was supportive of the resistance, as many in our village were – and I got her silent consent to share some of our meager food allowance.

As I continued my daily walks to the woods, some of the villagers must have noticed what I was doing. And the men in hiding must have started feeling unsafe, too, for one evening, after nightfall, there was a knock on our door.

And there he stood – a tall, dark young man. He walked inside, looking behind him to make sure there was no one around, and my *astonished parents invited him to sit with us at the dinner table. A resistant fighter in our house – that was getting dangerous, but he knew that, and didn't stay long. He told us that he came from another distant village in another part of France. He said he was hiding with two other friends, and that they needed to move on. That they no longer felt safe hiding near our village. That the Germans would be there soon.*

He thanked us for our generosity and said they had to leave that night, but that he would be back after the war.

"The end of the war is near," he said.

And I believed him. As I accompanied him to the door, he held me in his arms, and promised he would be back for me. He left with a look in his eyes that still haunts me now as I think of it.

Shortly after he left, the Germans came. Someone must have reported on us, for they banged on our door and pulled us out of the house. They dragged me to the hideout in the forest and shoved me into that hole in the ground, the same hole where my resistant fighter hid with his friends. And they left me there to die.

I could see no further details, for Debbie took me through those painful memories quickly, as a good hypnotherapist does. But I knew they also killed my family, and that no one came to save me. I died in that hole in the ground.

I came back into the here and now with tears in my eyes.

"Do you recognize this man?" asked Debbie, and all I could do was nod.

Yes, I recognized him.

That young man, whose life I might have saved with my daily gifts of food, was the same man who saved my own life in another lifetime, the 18th century one. They shared the same soul, with a hundred years or so separating the two lifetimes. They even had the same dark eyes.

I did not know much about the French Resistance during the Second World War, so when I got back home I did some research, and learned that indeed, there were many resistance fighters – or Maquis. When I read about the Maquis, as the French Resistance fighters called themselves, it all sounded familiar – I had a strong feeling of déjà vu. Sure, perhaps I had seen a movie or read a book about them and had forgotten about it. Perhaps someone told me their story and it was erased from my mind, only to be remembered during a regression. But the emotions I felt were real – at least as strong and real as the emotions I feel on a daily basis. And the body memories were a powerful working tool to help bring back amazing details from the distant past.

Sixteen

am I my brother's keeper?

Here is another memory, or perhaps just a collection of images I had under hypnosis: *I am a child of five or six, a young boy. My home is a simple structure in the mountains of Tibet, or maybe Nepal. I have a sense of geographical location, but not the knowledge that comes with education. The sense of place is at once overwhelming and vague. I know where I am, but I can't express it in clear words.*

I can see myself in ragged clothes and torn shoes – shoes that have been patched up many times. I am happy and grateful to have these shoes; it is better than having no shoes at all. I wear them daily in the snowy mountain winter, and I am one of the lucky ones. Not only because of the shoes, but I am one of the lucky ones because I have love. My mother's love.

My mother and I live in a small stone structure, protected from the winds by a cliff on the mountainside. We have wool rugs on our earth floor, and the house is kept clean. Sometimes, when we can afford it, it is even kept warm. Most nights we sleep huddled together under wool blankets. I love my life.

But my life changes very suddenly, when my mother becomes ill. It is clear – at least to her – that she might die. I don't want to believe it.

She arranges for me to be sent to a monastery higher up in the mountains. She tells me I am to be educated there.

I don't want to leave her, but she tells me that we will see each other again, if not in this world, then in the next. And I am only six or seven years old, and take her word for it. I leave her bedside and clutch the hand of the man who is to take me to the monastery – this man is not someone from our family – for it is only my mother and me – but I know this man. He is someone from our village. I look at my mother's face for the last time before I depart, and my eyes fill with tears. I can feel them under my tightly shut eyelids.

I can also feel the fear – mixed with excitement – about the upcoming trip to the monastery. This kind acquaintance takes the trip with me, and hands me over to the head of the monastery – a man with intelligent eyes and an open, honest face. His head is shaved, his skin is radiant. He looks old to me, but must be forty at the most.

I am accepted as a novice, a monk in training. My head is now shaved too, so there is no telling me apart from the other boys there, except that I am probably the youngest.

Perhaps that is why he takes a liking to me, the head of the monastery who received me when I arrived. Or maybe he just feels sorry for me, for he knows I now have no one in the world but him. And he becomes my teacher, my mentor, my master, like the father I've never had, for I never knew who my real father was. My mother said he disappeared when I was a baby. She said he left one day on a trip across the mountains and never returned.

For years to come, I am an apprentice. I am pleased to be running little services for the head of the monastery, for my mentor. I am sometimes allowed to sit at his feet and silently listen to his words of wisdom when people come to him to seek them. When he is invited to perform rituals at distant villages, he often takes me with him. I feel appreciated and loved once again.

Memories of my mother slowly fade away, and when word arrives of her death some months later, I cry. I am sad for many days, but I then become totally absorbed in my daily chores at the monastery, by the long hours of work and prayer.

I become even closer to my master, my teacher, my lama. When he breaks the news of my mother's death to me, he assures me that I will see her again in another time and place. I believe him.

I learn to make myself invisible on the many occasions when I am allowed to accompany my teacher, and feel proud when asked to perform one errand or another on his behalf. I became an expert at serving tea to him and the guests that come to the monastery from faraway to see him. I brew the tea from herbs I collect in spring and summer and dry for use during the cold winter months.

As my limbs stretch and my voice grows thicker, I am assigned more and more duties at the monastery. I am taught to read and write and to draw beautiful characters in calligraphy. I am able to recite many mantras, and I am asked to teach them to others.

I have this picture in my mind: a boy in brownish-crimson robes, rushing with a small wooden tray in his hands. He is going to serve his master and a group of important guests. The boy's cheekbones are high, his skin smooth, his head closely shaved. This is me.

I can still feel the gratitude in my heart, gratitude towards this man who took me in as a helpless child, and watched me grow into an agile adolescent. I see more images, colorful and clear in my mind's eye: stone walls that contain the world I know. Set on a mountaintop, the scenery around me is rocky and bare. I feel at home here, I feel safe. I never want to leave this place – and I don't. I am ordained as a monk, devoted to the quiet routine and the peace of mind I find, and I spend the rest of my life at the monastery. I am happy there; I am respected. And when my master, my beloved teacher, dies, I know for sure we will meet again.

Before he dies, he says that I should take his place as the one in charge of the monastery. I must be in my early thirties now, I've spent more than twenty years learning from my master, and he has taught me well. He had inspired me to show kindness to all living creatures, he had shown me that the world can be a good place.

I miss him when he is gone, but I am grateful to have had him in my life.

As the regression session winds down, I am slowly coming back to the here and now, but the images in my mind are powerful and moving.

"Do you recognize anyone from that life in your current life?" asks my regression therapist, my colleague Caroline.

"Yes, I do," I say, hardly able to contain the tears freely flowing down my cheeks.

"I recognize my teacher. He is my brother Michael."

This regression session has stayed with me for many days, as I was trying to understand what there was to learn from it. Was Michael really my teacher, my mentor in another life? And is it possible, is it possible at all, that we have met again in this life – me as an older sister, him as my baby brother – only so he could leave so soon, and teach me and the rest of the family further lessons?

I have learned so much since his death, things I would have probably not encountered otherwise, not with such intensity. In this life, Michael's death has taught me patience, has taught me acceptance, has guided me towards what is so important in my life now.

He has gently pushed me towards a spiritual path – the spiritual aspect of my being, which meant so much to me when I was younger, before I got sidetracked by career and family and life in general.

Does it matter if he really was my teacher and master in a monastery in Tibet or Nepal hundreds of years ago? Not to me. The experience under hypnosis was powerful, and the affect is one of deeper acceptance and understanding of the difficulties life has put in my way. It took me one step further towards coping and accepting my brother's death.

Seventeen

on mediumship and free will

The true pioneers of spirit work are ancient tribesmen, who danced around the fire in a trance while communicating with the spirits of their ancestors. All that is very nice, but it doesn't always go down well with the inhabitants of our modern society, to which I take pride in belonging.

So I started searching for pioneering work of modern men and women who achieved more or less the same result as our more animate forefathers, but who did it in such a way that can also appeal to the educated and rational minds of present day women and men.

While I'd personally happily attend a shamanic journeying workshop or a tarot reading session just for the experience and fun of it, I realize that there are others who would be put off by such a show. Many search for what they refer to as 'more scientific proof' or 'rational proof' of the existence of spirits, the eternity of the soul and the possibility of communication between the two worlds – ours and theirs.

Scientists are the first to admit that there is very little in our world that science can currently explain – and this is not because its methods are flawed – but because it does not have all the right tools and information – yet.

I sympathize with those who like to have scientific, or at least rational, proof – as I am one of them. It's not that I don't have faith in the spirit world – I do – but faith has never been jeopardized by having further proof.

I found some satisfying circumstantial evidence in the first three books Dr. Michael Newton wrote – *Journey of Souls, Destiny of Souls* and *Life Between Lives: Hypnotherapy for Spiritual Regression*. I gulped them down as if they were gusts of fresh air after I had been stuck in a stuffy room for years. Dr. Michael Newton is an American psychologist, hypnotherapist and a pioneer in the area of research of the afterlife, or what he calls 'Life Between Lives' (LBL). He did many years of clinical research of 'soul memories' of his clients, under deep hypnosis, and published many case studies in these books. They are written in a clear and flowing language – destined to be read by everyone and not just by professional therapists.

His first two books, *Journey of Souls* and *Destiny of Souls*, have truly transformed the way I look at life. Not only that many details described in them as memories of patients during his over-thirty-years of work as a hypnotherapist and collecting case studies made sense to me, they actually felt familiar. I thought that was uncanny, and immediately recommended the books to friends and family. Most of them expressed no interest in reading them, which to me was another surprising revelation: many people say they want evidence to the existence of an afterlife, but when you try to provide it, they are too busy to look at it.

Admittedly, we all have busy lives. That's why we are here – to live them to the fullest. But we are talking of an afterlife here – something eternal. I was amazed that most people couldn't spare a few hours of reading to educate themselves more on the subject, but are so quick to dismiss the possibility of our being eternal souls who reincarnate in human bodies, again and again, until we reach enlightenment.

Dr. Michael Newton's books were just the beginning of an emerging pattern. I'd find another piece of evidence, or just interesting information, which I wanted to share with family and friends, and with few exceptions, I've found disinterest. More than that – I've often encountered fear.

We've been so indoctrinated by our society to fear death, ghosts, the possibility of an afterlife and anything we don't know enough about – that it is very difficult to get beyond that fear. In societies where spirits and death are intertwined in daily life, there is perhaps less difficulty to discuss these issues. But in our society, I've found that discussing these subjects with people might cause them to dismiss you, or to fear you.

So at some point, I made a conscious choice not to hide who I was, and what had become so important in my life – and let the people who were put off by this, go, if they so wished. Over the years, this has probably cost me a few friends, but others came in their stead – people with whom I have more in common and who understand more about who I am now.

As I delved in deeper into contact with the Other Side I realized that just like us, souls on the 'other side of life' are going through developmental challenges. As most of us can't (or won't) talk directly to those who are on the other side, some people choose to go to mediums – and for millennia, mediums have acted as intermediaries between the two worlds.

I've often wondered what it was that mediums did and what it took to be, or become one. I thought of going to see a medium many times, in order to satisfy that curiosity, but felt reluctant to do it because of how society around me viewed the whole subject of mediumship. Mediums are often portrayed as gypsy ladies with big gold earrings and a crystal ball or as fantasists or con-artists that are after their clients' money. That was not the kind of experience I was looking for.

But I now realized that mediums are not witches or wizards; neither are they all con artists (although, like in every profession, some might be doing things for the wrong reasons or in an unprofessional manner).

Mediums are simply channels, people who mediate between our world and 'the other world', or between the spirits of the living and the spirits of the dead. Although some mediums are born with this talent and don't have to work hard to develop it, others can tune themselves in and learn, by practice, how to use this ability, which seems to be built into every human being.

I was always very much in tune with messages that were meant for me personally – such as whether to trust a certain person or not, to go to a specific place or not, or to engage in a certain activity. I followed these hunches throughout my life, thinking of them as mere intuition or 'gut feelings'. I found that following them made my life easier, richer, more interesting. However, I was not in tune with messages destined for others.

In fact, even on the occasions I thought I did get a 'gut feeling' or a 'message' for someone else, especially after someone close to them had died, I never allowed myself to tell them about it. It just didn't feel right – how do I know if what I sensed was for real? How do I know if and how this will influence their lives – and why should I take this responsibility? I was always taught that you don't give advice when you're not asked for it, and I tried to follow this practice all my life. However, the difference was that these 'gut feelings' didn't really feel as if they were coming from inside – as if they were *my* advice that *I* wanted to give. They were more like bits of 'knowing' that suddenly popped into my head, uninvited.

I later learned that a good medium can take themselves – their opinions, their judgments – completely out of the picture when tuning into messages from beyond.

While their judgment is necessary in order to determine whether the information they get is from a reliable source (for spirits, just like living people, vary in their degree of reliability and trustworthiness – hence many mediums learn to work with spirits they know and trust), once this information comes through, the medium becomes no more than a channel for transferring the information to its destination.

In the *Book on Mediums* by French writer Allan Kardec (pseudonym of teacher and educator Hippolyte Leon Denizard Rivail, who lived and worked in the early–mid 19th century and authored five books of spiritist codification, for which he is known as 'the systematiser of spiritism'), one can find much information on the subject of mediums and the spirits they work with.

This *Book on Mediums* is essentially a training manual for mediums, full of information supposedly channeled from spirits.

This book discusses, among other things, the connection between a medium and his or her advising spirits and different situations which mediums can and do face, as well as general observations that – like most of those that come across from the spirit world – can be quite confusing. They tend to be general and can often be interpreted in more than one way – because they are not supposed to dictate a certain path, only to point out the different paths that are available. They are meant to remind people of their life missions and developmental goals, as well as of a very important universal law – the exercise of free will.

Free will is something that is of great importance when discussing spirituality, because people often wonder if some things in their lives are their 'destiny', if they are predetermined in any way. Once experiencing past life regressions, it is interesting to contemplate the possibility that many of the things in our lives are indeed pre-decided – by us. This can change the way we look at our lives, but it is important to remember that even when contracts are made in the spirit world, and when we have decided on a path we'd like to take in life, we can still change our minds by exercising our free will.

This is also the reason that if we'd like to have help from the spirit world, or would like to be able to connect to the world beyond our own, we need to actually *intend* to do it and *ask* to be able to do it. Otherwise, if it just 'happens' to us, it would deny us of our right to exercise our free will.

The difference between channeling positive spirits and less positive ones is also discussed in the *Book on Mediums*. The more experienced spirits (that come from higher levels) have noble intentions of helping people's development and aiding them on their life journeys and in difficult situations. The less experienced spirits, just like some humans that have not progressed very far in their developmental journeys, have their less noble agendas and don't care very much about helping others. I was intrigued to read the following observation, apparently channeled from the spirit world ('we' being the spirits communicating with the medium, or the channel):

> Good spirits are mainly influenced, in regard to a medium, by the use he makes of his faculty. We abandon the medium who uses his faculty for frivolities, or for the furtherance of ambitious designs, or if he refuses the exercise of his faculty for the convincing of those who seek his aid, or who need to witness our manifestations in order to acquire conviction. God has not granted this faculty to a medium merely for his own pleasure, and, still less, to subserve his ambition, but as a means of aiding his own advancement and that of his fellow men. If a spirit sees that a medium no longer subserves his intentions, and does not profit by his instructions and advice, he withdraws from him, and seeks someone more worthy of his assistance.
>
> (*Book on Mediums*, chapter 17, paragraph 220).

Just like there are unpleasant and negative living people, there are unpleasant and negative dead people. The dead negative ones should not be treated any differently from the live ones – it is simply best to avoid or ignore them.

I've since learned that most unhappy people, and most unhappy spirits, have turned this way because they haven't experienced enough love and acceptance in their lifetime.

While developing my ability of mediumship, I've had some experiences that convinced me that most unpleasant spirits are actually sad spirits, and with a bit of patience and understanding one can find the good in them, too – just like one can find some good in every person.

Eighteen

further proof

We were told to bring some spoons and forks to the last session of our Regression Therapy training, so I chose some from a set we no longer used, and packed them in my bag.

I felt a strong burst of anticipation and excitement as I boarded the plane for this trip to England. Firstly, I was heavily pregnant – eight and a half months, to be exact. When I learned on the very day of my 40th birthday that I was pregnant with my third child, I was surprised for it was not a planned pregnancy. It was more of a 'if it happens then great' kind of pregnancy. I did very much want to finish my Regression Therapy training, so when I learned I was pregnant I started calculating the due date, to know whether I would be able to complete my training. To my amazement, I learned that I would be able to complete it just in time for the birth, as if this whole thing has been planned by a meticulous planner on an invisible calendar.

In fact, that week was the very last one I would legally be able to fly back – so if there was a two-day delay for some reason, I thought to myself, I might have to stay in the UK and give birth there. So I even looked up on the internet and noted the number of the nearest hospital with a maternity unit, just in case.

Secondly, the main topics of the last Regression Therapy module were Spirit Release and Inner Child Healing – both areas of much interest to me, and I looked forward to learning more about them.

And then there was the spoon and fork thing.

The fact that I was at the end of my eighth month of pregnancy with my third child only added to my excitement and commitment – I wanted to finish the course before I gave birth, because I knew that once I did, with two other young boys at home, I'd have other things on my mind for a while. However, my newfound path seemed to have affected every single aspect of my life, including my pregnancy.

Through daily exercises of meditation and self-hypnosis (which in reality are not very different from one another) I was able to enjoy a relaxed, uneventful pregnancy.

When I was pregnant with my second baby in 2005, I heard someone mention a birthing technique called 'HypnoBirthing®'. I was always curious about hypnosis but had never experienced it, except watching a couple of television shows where the hypnotist seemed to help people make fools of themselves in front of a large audience, and I was not impressed.

However, HypnoBirthing sounded as if it was something totally different. I heard it was an empowering method to allow women to go within and give birth in a calm and relaxed way, wherever they chose to give birth – at a hospital, maternity clinic or at home. I decided to take a HypnoBirthing course with an American instructor who was teaching in Paris, where I resided at the time, and was surprised to discover that what I thought of as a mystical and even somewhat frightening thing was really no more than very deep relaxation, putting our conscious mind on 'the back burner' as we often do when reading a book, watching a movie or even when we drive somewhere familiar and just get there without thinking about it too much.

Our conscious mind likes to control our lives – to analyze constantly and think things through, but when we learn to relax it, our brain works on different waves. As we all know, our brain is made up of billions of neurons, which use electricity to communicate with each other. This electrical activity in the brain can be detected and measured with special medical equipment, and different patterns of brain waves exist in different states of consciousness.

When we are alert in our everyday lives, our brain emits Beta frequency waves (13 to 60 pulses a second in the Hertz scale). When we are relaxed – physically and mentally – but aware of what is happening around us, our brain emits Alpha wave frequency (7 to 13 pulses per second). This is the best frequency to learn new information, such as new languages.

When we are nearly asleep, or in a state of hypnosis or deep meditation, Theta waves can be measured – at 4 to 7 pulses per second, and when we are unconscious, in deep sleep or in catalepsy (muscular rigidity – a test often used in hypnosis to see whether the subject is relaxed before entering an hypnotic trance), Delta waves can be measured, between 0.1 and 4 cycles per second.

The most amazing thing about all the information above is that we can learn to control, or at least to influence, our brain waves.

When contemplating the upcoming birth, I knew without any doubt that I wanted to try to experience a non-medicated birth, this time at home if the situation permitted. While my first two births were in clinics in Paris, these were both clinics that promoted 'natural birthing' and only midwives attended the delivery if all went well – and in my case, it did.

My doctor was happy with the way things were going (although, as many doctors, was not thrilled about the prospect of a home birth), so I hired a midwife who would deliver the baby and started re-reading Marie Mongan's book *HypnoBirthing®*. In it there are many exercises and relaxation techniques and meditations – explained in clear and concise language – clear even to those who have never considered hypnosis before.

Throughout my pregnancy – and especially as I was nearing its end – I was surprised to realize that my baby was responding to many suggestions I'd made during these relaxation exercises, such as turning head down in preparation for delivery, communicating through little kicks and squirms and more.

Many of my friends had expressed their concerns for my home-birthing prospects, and their doubts about my hypnosis birthing theories. By now I had gotten so used to these doubts that they didn't bother me very much – I was confident that I was doing the right thing for me and my baby.

As all was well, and my due date a little over a month away, I got the required medical certificate to fly from Geneva to the UK. Full of excitement and anticipation for the course, spoons and forks safely packed in my luggage, I headed for Dorset.

The course itself was fascinating – we learned more Spirit Release techniques and worked with our Inner Child – the young person that is within us all and often carries scars from events that have long gone. These are all topics that I could write pages and pages about, but it was not them – nor the many bonding experiences I had with my unborn baby during the course – that truly changed the way I perceive things.

Yes, by now I believed that there was an afterlife. I even now truly believed in past lives. I was also confident that death was not The End, The Final Chapter, but merely the beginning of another adventure.

But what made an enormous difference, what made the final penny drop, was the last evening's spoon and fork session, my final evening at Gaunts House.

We had gathered in the main room, clutching our forks and spoons. We were about to try bending them – not with force, but with energy.

Even if by now I believed in the afterlife, I did not really believe I could bend spoons – for I am no Uri Geller. Of course, I'd seen it done on television; I'd read about it; and I thought of it as a magician's trick. But I was still excited about trying.

We all sat in a circle around the room, each clutching a spoon or a fork. I had one of each.

"Forks are more fun," said Hazel, Andy's co-instructor,

"because we can also bend each prong individually."

I chose a spoon to start with. If I could bend that, it would be good enough for me.

"OK," said Andy. "Choose the spot you plan to bend the spoon or fork at, and concentrate on it, putting all your energy into that spot. Rub it slightly with one finger, very gently."

We all did as he said.

"Right," he said. "Now, let's try to forget about it completely. Now we need to raise the energy level in the room. Put your forks and spoons down and stand up."

We lay our cutlery on our chairs.

"Let's act silly now," said Andy. "Just have fun, and the main thing is, try to forget about bending the cutlery. We just need to have a good laugh and raise the energy vibrations."

I've since learned from experience that, indeed, laughter is a fantastic way to make energy vibrations higher. Often, it can be more efficient than hours of meditation.

We started hopping around the room like a bunch of drunken teenagers. We sang; we bounced around, occasionally bumping into each other; we made each other laugh.

My fellow Regression-Therapists-to-be passed by me in a circle of laughter; happy faces that I had learned to love and trust over the past year swung by me like a merry-go-round of shiny eyes. We had kept in touch through the weeks that passed between the various modules of the course, and now we suddenly realized that very soon we would be going our separate ways. So we enjoyed one of the last opportunities we had to have fun together, and we tried to forget about the forks and spoons silently waiting on our chairs. I can't say that I personally succeeded; it was always somewhere on the back of my mind.

"Now, quickly," said Andy. "Just go back to your forks and spoons, and bend them."

I rushed back to the spoon, picked it up and tried bending it.

We were told not to apply any force on it, so I didn't. It was supposed to just bend.

Nothing happened.

The cold metal lay still in my hand.

I knew I couldn't do it, I thought to myself.

I heard some cries of awe and raised my eyes to look around me. Some of the course participants actually held bent spoons in their hands. A couple even had forks with prongs sticking in different directions. How did they do that? Some of that cutlery looked as if it had been through a serious meltdown, and yet I knew very well that only moments before these were all perfectly usable spoons and forks.

"OK," said Andy. "Let's try again for those who didn't do it the first time."

We continued the hopping around and the singing for a few more minutes, and rushed towards our cutlery again. Some of the participants bent their spoons and forks even more. I didn't.

"There's no point in forcing it," said Andy to the few of us who looked utterly disappointed. "You really have to not think about it, to be able to let go, for it to succeed. Let's do something else now."

Hazel pulled out a pair of dowsing rods – a simple pair of L-shaped metal rods. These rods are held one in each hand, with the short arm of the L held upright and the longer arm horizontal. When something is found, the rods cross over one another, making an x.

"OK," said Andy. "I need two volunteers to leave the room."

Half-a-dozen hands rose up in the air and Hazel picked a couple of people – Laura and John – who left the room. Andy proceeded to building an imaginary 'energy wall' across the room. He told us where this wall would be, and we all concentrated on it, imagining it standing before us.

"When a group of people concentrates on something," said Andy, "it makes the vibrations stronger."

"You can call one of them back inside," said Andy to Hazel, and she did.

Laura came back in, holding her dowsing rods. She stood silently at one end of the long room and started advancing slowly, step by step, holding the two rods in front of her like a cowboy advancing for a shootout, pistols at the ready. For a few moments nothing happened.

Then the rods crossed.

"Here?" she asked hesitantly. "Is this where you've put the energy wall across the room?"

It was.

"Can you call John to come back in?" asked Andy, and someone went out to get him.

He repeated the same exercise, walking slowly from the end of the room towards our imaginary wall.

And he walked straight through it.

Everyone laughed.

"Oh," he said. "Did I miss it?"

"You did," said Andy. "But that's OK. This is not an exact science, and like everything else in life, it takes practice."

That was an important lesson to me, because I've always thought: *either you've got it, or you haven't.*

Now I know this is not true.

Sensitivity to energy, like any other talent such as being good at music or at a sport, can be a gift someone is born with. But it can also be developed, with practice and dedication.

We proceeded to sensing each other's energy fields, or auras, with the dowsing rods. An amazing thing happened when Andy wanted to demonstrate to us the power of positive versus negative thinking.

Two people stood apart from each other, and one tried to sense the energy field of the other with help of the dowsing rods. The dowsing rods started crossing when the person holding them approached the other, standing person.

"Now step back again, and the standing person should think something very positive about someone, anyone," said Andy.

When the person standing still thought positive thoughts, the dowsing rods started crossing in the hands of the person holding them when they were much farther away from the standing person. It was as if the energy field of the standing person grew, expanded.

"Now step back, and the standing person – think something really negative about someone," instructed Andy.

When the standing person did so and the one holding the rods approached them, the dowsing rods did not start crossing until they were only a meter or so away – showing how the energy field had actually shrunk. It was quite amazing to watch. Then we all took turns in trying this experiment.

This was another important lesson I've learned that evening – negative thoughts about someone else actually affect the person thinking them negatively.

Then Andy demonstrated how holding a mobile phone can cause the energy field to shrink. It was pretty amazing to watch the dowsing rods signaling the edge of the energy field of the person holding the mobile phone cross less than a meter from their body, while before they crossed when three or four meters away.

But my main lesson was yet to come.

We decided to finish that inspiring evening with another energy exercise – an energy pyramid. We all put our hands up, holding them together in the center of a circle, creating a cone shape, and two people sat underneath. We all chanted a deep 'Om' several times, and the people sitting inside our pyramid reported that the feeling was fantastic – energizing and relaxing at once.

We then switched places, taking turns again, so that everyone got their turn in experiencing the energy vibrations inside the pyramid. I was one of the last people to have a go, together with two other participants.

"Ommmmmm…" buzzed the energy around me, and I closed my eyes and surrendered to the electrifying sensation that went through my body.

Then the chanting died down slowly and everyone put their hands down. We looked at each other, tired but exhilarated. Some very powerful things had happened in the room over the past couple of hours.

"Bedtime," someone said.

I had the same thought, but just then, I had another.

I rushed to my spoon, still waiting perfectly straight on my chair. When I touched it, it felt warm. I tried to bend it with two fingers, the slightest pressure – and it felt as if it turned into liquid in my hand. I could hardly believe what I was feeling. It felt like warm dough, like modeling clay. And it bent easily.

I then picked up my fork and tried to bend it. It, too, felt soft and warm. It bent as if it was a piece of rubber.

I looked around me to see what everyone else was doing – they were saying good night to each other, getting ready to leave the room.

"Look," I called out and waved my cutlery in the air. "Look, I've just bent these!"

The few people who had not managed to bend their spoons and forks earlier tried again. And with the exception of one or two people, they all watched in amazement as their cutlery easily bent in their hands!

Once in bed, my mind was buzzing. I was too thrilled to fall asleep. I clutched my bent spoon and fork and could not let go of a thought that accompanied me through most of that night: *If metal can really be bent with the power of energy, by pure thought, imagine what else the power of the mind can achieve.*

I finally managed to fall asleep, and when I awoke the next

morning at six, ready to go down for a session of meditation, I knew I would never again doubt the power of thought.

I have since practiced bending forks and spoons after meditating, when feeling that there was a high energy around and even in a restaurant once, just after our entire table (of six) burst into laughter. While harnessing laughter as a mean to raise your vibration might seem silly and unserious, it is actually a wonderful way to go about it. So feel free to laugh away next time you want to try something spiritual – and you, too will be able to attest to the wonderfully elevating power of laughter.

How To 5: bending spoons

Pick a spoon that is neither too sturdy, nor too flimsy. Just a normal spoon from a set you no longer need – but definitely not the very cheap kind that you can bend easily anyway!

Hold the spoon in your hand, and make the intent to bend it at a specific spot. Usually the 'weakest spot' of a spoon is just where the neck connects to the handle. After making the intent and holding it for a minute or so, put the spoon aside.

Now comes the hardest part: not thinking about it. You need to focus on raising your energy level, trying to forget all about the spoon you'd like to bend.

There are two easy ways to do this. One is meditation. Meditate for twenty minutes or so, without thinking about the spoon at all. Easier said than done, but as you get better at meditating, you should be able to empty your mind from all thoughts.

Another fun way to raise your energy level is laughing – but this is hard to achieve on your own. You need to find, perhaps with a friend or two, a good reason to laugh from your bottom of your heart – the kind of laughter that takes over you and leaves you teary-eyed. This can very quickly raise your energy vibration and is a very powerful way to achieve many things, including bending cutlery. Perhaps you can invite a few like-minded friends over to have a good time – rent your favorite comedies, tell jokes or do anything else that will help you all have a good laugh.

Once you've raised your energy level, go back to your spoon. Pick it up and don't even think about it – just bend it. When your vibrations are high, the metal spoon will feel like warm liquid in your hands. It is an amazing sensation, and well worth practicing in order to be able to experience it. Once you've achieved it with a spoon, try it with a fork! Then you can even bend each prong of the fork individually…

The most important part about this exercise is – have fun! It is not a test, but merely a way to prove to yourself (and to others if you so wish) that 'thought energy' can have a manifestation in the physical world. This of course can be implemented on many things – a job you'd like to get, a test you'd like to pass. Use the same technique – make the conscious intent by making a wish out loud, writing it down or asking for the help of your higher self or your spirit guide. Then forget about it. If you can raise your energy levels, you will be amazed at how many intents you have set can manifest in the physical world.

Bending spoons: quick guide

1 Pick a spoon that is neither too sturdy, nor too flimsy.
2 Make the conscious intent to bend it in a specific spot. Concentrate on this spot for a minute or two.
3 Now let go of this intent, and try to forget about it. You need to raise your energy level.
4 Meditate for twenty minutes or so, or find a way to have a really good laugh, on your own or with a few friends.
5 Go back to your spoon, pick it up and without giving it a second thought, just bend it.
6 It didn't work? Try raising your energy level some more. If it still doesn't work, just let it go and try it another time, when you don't feel the pressure to succeed. The more you manage to let go, the easier it will be to bend the spoon.
7 Once you've managed to bend a spoon, try bending a fork. Those are generally sturdier and harder to bend – but you can also try bending each prong individually.
8 Most important: have fun. This exercise is not a competition of any kind, merely a way to give yourself further proof that thought energy has manifestations in the physical world.

How To 6: dowsing

Dowsing rods have certainly been used for hundreds of years, and probably for much longer. The art of dowsing has survived mockery, scorn and religious zeal. And it often works. Unsure about this? Why not just give it a try? After all, nowadays dowsers are employed by water, mineral, precious metals and oil companies, by diamond and mining companies and even by the police, to work in crime scenes. Many of these employers fear ridicule and keep the fact that they employ dowsers very quiet. But still, if nothing else, it might save you hours of looking for lost objects around the house.

Dowsing can be done by using Y or L shaped twigs, or modern metal dowsing rods, which are usually L shaped. Dowsing for information is not much different from using a pendulum, as the principle is very similar. *Field dowsing* – e.g. looking for water or minerals – is usually done when the person is in the field and physically near the object of the search.

As with the pendulum, and with bending spoons – intent is crucial. You have to make your intent clear – what are you looking for? Is it your keys? Is it a leak in a pipe?

Then you hold the dowsing rods by their longer part if they are L shaped or Y shaped – one in each hand if you have two rods, or both hands on the longer bar if you have a Y shaped rod, and you wait.

Take a deep breath, focus your mind on the questions, and advance slowly. As you approach what you are looking for, the rods will start moving on their own, signaling you are near your target. You might have to pace back and forth a few times, and again to confirm the exact location especially if you plan to dig a well in your back garden, for example.

There are many explanations for this phenomenon, but mine is quite simple: the rods are a tool. The real work is done by the handler's consciousness, or 'higher self', and the more you are connected to your this consciousness, the more you can suspend disbelief and just let yourself be guided by the information you receive, the better dowser you will be. Some of us are born with small antennas, some are born with larger ones. But we can all work on developing what some people prefer to call a 'sixth sense', and I like to call 'our receiving devices'. Try it just for fun – what is there to lose?

Dowsing: quick guide

1 As with any spiritual work, your intent is the most important thing. Define it clearly. What are you hoping to achieve in this dowsing session?

2 Ask for guidance. In the spiritual world, you need to ask in order to get assistance, as your guides do not want to interfere with your free will.

3 Hold your dowsing rods gently, one in each hand, and take a few deep breaths. Don't grasp them too tight, or they will not be able to move.

4 Empty your minds from thoughts, and focus on your breathing or on the rods. They should feel as if they are an extension of your arms.

5 Start pacing slowly, paying attention to the movement of the rods. If they start moving or spinning, slow down. You are getting close to your target.

6 You will probably have to go over a specific area more than once, to get accurate information from the dowsing rods.

7 Most important: practice this skill without putting any pressure on yourself to succeed. The less stressed you are, the better it will work.

How To 7: affecting your energy field

This is a fun experiment, which I learned from my Regression Therapy teacher Andy Tomlinson. It is meant to give us some further proof about how various things affect our energy field – our aura. There are several stages to this experiment – but they are all straightforward and require very little preparation. However, you will need a friend who is willing to work with you, dowsing rods and a mobile phone.

Stage one: measuring a friend's energy field
Ask your friend to stand across the room, at least three meters (ten feet) away from you, preferably more. Imagine a protective bubble of white light around both of you, and ask for guidance. Set the intent as finding the edge of your friend's energy field.

Hold the dowsing rods, one in each hand. Take a few deep breaths and try to clear your mind from thoughts. Start walking slowly towards your friend, paying attention to the movement of your dowsing rods. Once they start moving or spinning, you have reached the edge of your friend's energy field. The size of the energy field varies between people, the time of day and the health and emotional state of the person – so don't be surprised if one day the energy field is larger or smaller than the next.

Stage two: measuring the effect of mobile phones on your energy field
After you've measured your friend's energy field, as him or her to hold a mobile phone in their hand. Try measuring the edge of their energy field while they are holding the mobile phone – you will probably find that it has shrunk quite a lot. Once I'd done this experience myself and realized what mobile phones do to our energy field, I made a habit of putting my phone on airplane mode most of the time. I turn it on when I need to use it and then turn it off or to airplane mode again. This, of course, is a personal

choice and is not compatible with everyone's priorities and lifestyle.

Stage three: measuring the effect of positive and negative thinking on your energy field

Go back to the beginning, standing at least three feet away from your friend, and holding your dowsing rods.

Ask your friend to think about someone or something that makes them feel good, or someone they love. Measure their energy field using the dowsing rods. You will probably find that their energy field has grown.

Now ask your friend to think negative thoughts about someone, or something they dislike. Measure their energy field again. You will probably find that it has shrunk considerably.

Then switch places, and ask your friend to repeat the above experiments on your energy field.

It was amazing for me to have this further proof that positive and negative thinking have such a powerful effect on us – and this experiment has helped me practice positive thinking in most areas of my life.

Of course, you can try to measure the effect of various things on your energy field – it is a fun and inspiring exercise. Enjoy!

Affecting an energy field: quick guide

1 Ask your friend to stand across the room, at least three meters (ten feet) away from you, preferably more.
2 Imagine a protective bubble of white light around both of you.
3 Ask for guidance.
4 Set the intent as finding the edge of your friend's energy field.
5 Hold the dowsing rods, one in each hand.

6 Take a few deep breaths and try to clear your mind from thoughts.

7 Start walking slowly towards your friend, paying attention to the movement of your dowsing rods.

8 Once they start moving or spinning, you have reached the edge of your friend's energy field.

9 Switch places – and ask your friend to measure your energy field, repeating instructions 1–8.

10 To measure the effect of mobile phones on your energy field, or on your friend's energy field, repeat stages 1–8 while the person whose field is being measured holds a mobile phone (which is switched on!).

11 To measure the effect of positive and negative thoughts on your energy field, or on your friend's energy field, repeat stages 1–8 while the person whose field is being measured thinks positive thoughts, and then the second time around think positive thoughts.

12 Most important: keep an open mind, try not to be emotionally involved and this experiment – and have fun!

Nineteen

death and (re)birth

Many people consider dying to be a traumatic event. It certainly can be for family and friends who stay behind on the earth plane. But for the concerned person, it may be a much more pleasant event than birth.

Consider these two different scenarios – death and birth – while agreeing to put aside all doubts about reincarnation for the duration of reading these lines:

When death is sudden, there is usually no pain involved. The spirit often leaves the body even before the actual death occurs, because of the shock – and it is suddenly free. No more constraints, no more physical needs. A body is nice to have, but it comes with many limitations that the spirit does not adhere to. It feels wonderful – although possibly disconcerting at first – to be free of these limitations.

For someone who has never even considered the possibility of their spirit being a separate entity, something totally separate from their physical body, this can be a scary experience.

Where do they go? What do they do next? Perhaps the answer to that is not always obvious, which is why some spirits remain earth-bound for a while. They are worried about leaving their familiar surroundings, and going someplace different. This is probably the case with young souls, who have not been through death and rebirth many times.

For those who've been there before many times, it is not a complicated procedure.

Yes, there are the family and friends who are left behind, and the deceased may wonder – *will they be all right without me?* The answer is that in the long-term, they always will be.

And once we've accepted this newly found freedom, we can

then continue our journey into the spirit realm and embrace this understanding that we are eternal beings; that life on earth was one act in a multi-act play.

Family and friends who stay behind will grieve; they will miss us. But we now know the truth: we shall meet again, and they do have their own journey to complete. We are not responsible for their happiness and well-being. They are responsible for their own. They might even learn a lesson or two – perhaps even a difficult one – from our departure. But in the end, the difficult lessons are often the most important ones.

We are now able to head towards the light that is always there for us; join our spirit family; enjoy unconditional love and acceptance and to free ourselves from the constraints and difficulties of having a human body. We can learn many new things, until we are ready to incarnate and inhabit a human body again. All is well.

Now let's consider birth.

We've spent some time in the spirit realms, got used to the lightness and freedom that comes with living in such a different dimension. We know we are eternal beings, even if we may forget that soon. Now we are heading back to the earth plane, for another life.

We get a body – a baby's body – which takes some getting used to. We emerge through what can sometimes be a stressful event – a difficult birth, stressed mother, unfamiliar surroundings. We might still remember where we came from, but this memory is now slowly fading away. Some studies have shown that children up to the age of two can still remember details from before their birth – but these are quickly forgotten once they are discouraged from talking about such things.

In societies where reincarnation is regarded as a normal belief, there are many more reported cases of children talking about their past lives. In Druze communities, which reside mostly in Syria, Lebanon and Israel, children who remember their past-life families are not regarded as very unusual. Being a sect that emerged during the 11th century from Ismailism – a branch of shia Islam – they are often weary of sharing these stories with people outside their religious community for fear of being prosecuted. Hindus and Buddhists regard reincarnation as a matter of fact – and the human body is treated as a vessel for the soul, and therefore can be disposed of by cremation once the soul had left it. In Hindu traditions, the reason for destroying the human body after death is to induce a feeling of detachment into the disembodied spirit – for apparently, many spirits initially feel reluctant to leave their newly deceased body, and hang around it for a while. The destruction of the human body will encourage the spirits to pass to 'the other world' – where they belong.

Being reborn is not as easy as departing, and obviously also depends on the circumstances into which the baby is born. The circumstances, in their turn, depend on the lessons that need to be learned from that specific life. So there is no way to know where we are heading during a specific life – other than looking deep inside and listening to our intuition, gut-feelings, instincts, memories, messages from 'the other side' or whatever we prefer to call this information.

Human life can be – and often is – stressful. Death is not. So why are we so afraid of it? And why are we so reluctant to allow our loved ones to continue their journey when their time comes? This has to do more with preconceived ideas in Western society, and with the (sometimes selfish) desire to keep our loved ones with us until we ourselves depart, for they bring much joy to our lives, and we miss them when they are gone.

But if we took a few moments to consider them and their best interests, more often than not, letting the dying person go peacefully, without 'hanging on' to them psychologically and energetically, would be the best for them, for the continuation of their journey, and even for those of us staying behind on the earth-plane.

How to: 8: assisting death or birth

(DISCLAIMER: THIS DOES NOT CONSTITUTE MEDICAL ADVICE)

Death

It is not often that we get to assist a death, but it can happen. If you do happen to find yourself in a situation where you are with a dying person, you can help in several ways:

1 Provide reassurance that it is all right, they do not have to be afraid.

2 Help them understand that you love them and will miss them, but that if they need to go, they can do so. Many people hold on to life and suffer physically because they are worried that their loved ones will not be fine without them.

3 If they talk of seeing someone coming to get them, a deceased relative or friend, or a 'being of light', don't tell them they are losing their mind. They are probably right.

4 Read to them or talk to them about something uplifting, to help them leave in good spirits.

5 Know that you can talk to them in the hours and days after they died. They can probably still hear you.

Birth

Welcoming a soul into life can be one of the most uplifting experiences. Those who've attended births can testify that there is something magical, out-of-this-world happening in the moment a baby emerges into this world.

Although many births will inevitably be in hospitals and with medical assistance and/or interference, think about how you would have liked to be welcomed into this world. Consider the following:

1 Ask for dim lights if at all possible, rather than harsh hospital projectors.

2 Soft music would help make the transition – which can be scary for a newborn – especially if this is music they have heard before, while in the womb.

3 Communicate with the baby – asking him or her to emerge into this world in a calm way can have an amazing effect on the birthing process.

4 Ask him or her to tuck their chin in while sliding out through the birth canal.

5 Make them feel welcome from the moment they emerge – tell him or her how happy you are they've joined your life. Even if you think they cannot understand you – their soul can.

Although many think that newborns are not really aware of what is happening around them at the moment of birth, many hypnotic experiences have proved the contrary. People can be regressed to the moment of birth and even to the period in the womb – and many report specific memories, or even traumas from those periods.

The more welcome we can make a soul feel when they emerge into this world, the better chance we give them of a positive start to their journey.

Twenty

"we are with you"

My thoughts go back to the last time I went to Gaunts house.

"This might be silly," said Reena one evening as we sat together in one of the rooms. "But I have a message for you."

She closed her eyes, as if concentrating on the voices in her head.

"They tell me that whatever you are worried about, you shouldn't be. They say, *'we are with you on this'*."

"They are with me on what?" I asked, puzzled. I couldn't think of anything specific I was worried about.

"I don't know," said Reena. "But this is what I get. They say that they are with you on this."

"OK," I said. "Thanks."

Reena is one of the tutors I met along my journey. She is a wonderful young lady who does not call herself a medium, but does have regular contact with the world beyond. I was heavily pregnant, yet in very good health and spirits. I had a supportive family and an exciting time in my life. I had no real problems to complain of, and no burning need to ask questions of the spirit world.

There was one thing I could think of, that perhaps I was slightly worried about: I had given birth to my previous two boys at clinics, which encouraged natural birth. This time I wanted to give birth at home, but was somewhat worried as people around me kept telling me it was a foolish idea. What if something went wrong?

Still, it was something I had a desire to experience if all went well with my pregnancy.

Confident in my internal guidance and good health, as well as in my self-hypnosis techniques, I decided to have a home birth, and I did not take it lightly. I educated myself on what to do in case of emergency, I signed up for a place at the nearest hospital 'just in case' – and hired an experienced midwife.

Of course I was a little scared – everyone told me I should be – but I also knew that if all went as I had visualized it time and time again over the weeks before, then I would find it difficult to ever doubt again that energy, and thoughts, have power. It was almost like a deal I struck with the 'other side'.

"Help me go through with this, make it all go well, and I will forever believe not only in the power of thoughts, but also in the Other Side. I will no longer be afraid or embarrassed to tell other people about what I believe in."

Then, things unfold slightly differently from how I thought they might happen.

My husband is away with our youngest son on a school trip ten days before my due date.

"It's all fine," I reassure him. "I'll call you if I need you. I don't even have contractions."

My friend Miren volunteers to sleep over with her six-year-old boy, just in case.

"What are the chances that I will give birth in the one night my husband is away?" I tell everyone. "Don't worry, it'll be fine."

"Still, I'll feel better if Miren stays with you," says my husband. So Miren does.

My writer friends Katie and Paula come over for our monthly critiquing meeting. We skype, as usual, with our fourth writer friend, Jawahara, who now lives in the US. We spend the evening reading and commenting on each other's work, laughing and eating popcorn.

And the contractions start at midnight.

I don't want to wake my friend Miren up, or to call the midwife. I am feeling fine; the contractions are not regular, and not painful. I feel good. But I can't sleep.

It is as if time has become elastic again – the minutes and the hours trickle like sand in an hourglass. It is two o'clock in the morning, then three o'clock.

I try to relax, and visualize how all will be well. I feel I am not alone, and am grateful to my friend Miren for being around, even if asleep.

At four o'clock I decide to call the midwife, just in case. She had asked me to let her know when the contractions start, so she can get ready, although she lives only twenty minutes away.

"I am fine," I tell her. "My contractions are not regular, but I wanted to let you know that they've started."

"Very good," she says. "Let me know when you want me to come, when the contractions are painful or a bit closer together."

Another hour or so goes by, and the contractions get closer together. I rest between them, I meditate, and I feel the need for no one, for I am not alone. Indeed, I feel that "they are with me", whoever 'they' might be.

At a quarter to six I call the midwife again, for the contractions are a few minutes apart.

"I'm on my way," she says.

I waddle downstairs to prepare breakfast, in case my friend wakes up and cannot find the cereal or the bread.

Miren hears me fumbling around in the kitchen and emerges from her room, wild haired and wide-eyed.

"What's happening?" she asks.

"I just called the midwife," I say calmly. "She should be here any minute now."

Miren has already warned me that since she had a cesarean birth with her son Julian, she knows nothing about what to do if I do happen to give birth the one night she is on duty.

"Don't worry," I had said. "What are the chances this will happen that one specific night?"

Now she runs to get hot towels and water. She has no idea

what for, but she has seen it done in movies so it is the first thing that comes to her mind.

"Umm…never mind the hot water," I suddenly say, putting a packet of cereal down but holding on tightly to a spoon. "Can you help me get back to bed?"

She does, and within less than five minutes, at 6:03 am, my baby is born, sliding into this world as if he was always meant to be here, at this specific place and time. Our two boys sleep soundly, for there is no commotion, no noise, no stress.

The midwife arrives just in time to cut the umbilical cord, as if timed on an invisible stopwatch operated by an invisible hand. She hugs me and laughs.

"When you told me you will be practicing self-hypnosis, I had a feeling this baby might be born before I arrive," she said.

Miren is standing in the corner, pale. The midwife immediately enlists her help in measuring and weighing the baby. Our two boys continue sleeping soundly in their rooms and it is a magical moment for the four of us present.

Perhaps for all of those present, for I can still feel the presence of my invisible support crew in the room.

And still, I need one further piece of evidence, one further proof. I feel the energy in the room is high. And so I bend the spoon which I brought up from the kitchen earlier, and vow to look at it from then on every time I have a doubt about the power of energy and the world beyond ours.

Afterword

Four years have passed since my brother Michael died, and two years since I've finished my training as a Past Life Regression Therapist. It is merely the beginning of my spiritual journey – I know there will be more in the years to come.

One thing about opening my mind and my eyes to the world beyond ours is that it is a one-way street. I can never again say, "I didn't know".

Another thing is that the world around me seems to metamorphose – colors turn brighter, people turn more friendly, events seem to fall into place as if on their own. The magic of the journey is such that once one is no longer afraid to walk down this path – no matter how slow or how fast – the view on the way is stunning. Secrets unfold with every step and there is no need to prove anything to anyone – as each one of us walks at their own pace.

The fellow travelers on the path are always inspiring, and the difficulties challenging – but I know for a fact they will not stop me from progressing.

And last – but certainly not least – the messages I receive along the way, messages from the Other Side, multiply as I progress down my path. They are everywhere – in a song on the radio, a whisper in the wind or the words of a stranger. Open your ears, eyes and mind to the messages from your deceased loved ones, and you will hear, see and feel them. You don't need to go to a medium for contact with your deceased loved ones, you can just ask them to talk to you – in meditation, in your mind or in a dream. More often than not, they will.

I now believe my brother's death was not just 'an accident' that happened for no good reason. In fact, I believe that no death is. Our days in this life are always numbered, and when they reach their end – whether we've had a short life or a long one –

it's time to go back to the Other Side. This is not a bad thing for the person departing, although it is always difficult for those staying behind.

I do not wear large gold earrings and give people messages from their deceased relatives, but my contact with the Other Side is regular now. I know I am guided, but I do not talk of my guides, for they do not ask for recognition.

I can still only see a dragonfly, its wings as thin and light as silk and its body the color of rainbow. But on the wings of this dragonfly I take off and fly, for my soul carries no weight. It is our bodies – these borrowed vehicles of flesh and bone – that weigh us down. Our spirits are eternally free and invincible.

Recently, I went for a session with a healer who is also a medium. She put her hands over me and sensed my energy body, giving me whatever she thought was necessary. Forty minutes later, when I opened my eyes, she said to me, "You have a colorful cape around you that looks almost like wings. I have never seen such a thing."

I smiled to myself, then to her.

"It was a gift from a dragonfly," I said.

Acknowledgements

There are many people who inspired me to write this book, on this side of life, and on the other. I am grateful to them all.

My brother Michael, who continues his journey, has pointed me towards the right path. My grandmother Anna and grandfather Jacob, who have always been there for me, even after they've passed on.

My writer friends Roy York and Jean Currie, who have passed on, but keep providing constant guidance.

The wonderful people whom I've been lucky to share my life with and learn from – my mother Irina Shy and my two fathers, Harry Nadler and Ramy Shy. My other two brothers, Daniel and Gabriel, and my husband Richard and our three wonderful boys. Thank you for being in my life and for putting up with my writerly anomalies.

My writing mentor and friend Susan Tiberghien, and the three awesome writer divas: Katie Hayoz, Jawahara Saidullah and Paula Read. Your feedback is always invaluable. Thank you for your company on my journey.

My agents, Genevieve Carden, Jane Dystel and Miriam Goderich – I feel very fortunate to be working with you – it is always a joy.

The inspiring John Hunt and his team – Krystina Kellingley, Trevor Greenfeld, Maria Moloney, Mollie Barker, Nick Welch and Stuart Davies – thank you for believing in this book, and for doing something so innovative and forward thinking with John Hunt publishing. You are wonderful to work with.

My hypnosis and regression teachers and colleagues: Andy Tomlinson, Hazel Newton, Janet Treloar, Tatjana Radovanovic, Katherine Membery, Debbie Wild, Lorraine Flaherty and Aneta Zwawiak. I am so happy I had the chance to learn from you and to work together.

Souvenir Press for allowing me to reproduce the wonderful poem *Death is Nothing At All* by Canon Henry Scott-Holland, in this book.

And last but not least – the people whose presence in my life makes my journey more enjoyable – Celine, Helena, Corine, Kristina, Michelle, Jennifer, Ines, Stephanie, Anne, Daphna, Montse, Aneta, Sharon, Maayan, Jen, Michal, Yael, Hilit, Hannah, Saida, Katherine, Rachel, Miren, Marina, Shireen, Sandrine, Catherine, Isabelle, Gilles, Eric, Damien, Orian – so happy I get to share a part of my journey with you. I believe it is not a coincidence.

Further Reading

Bowman, C., *Children's Past Lives*, Element, 1998

Ewing, J., *Clearing: A Guide to Liberating Energies Trapped in Buildings and Lands*, Findhorn Press, 2006

Ewing, J., *Dreams of the Reiki Shaman: Expanding Your Healing Power*, Findhorn Press, 2011

Fontana, D., *Is There an Afterlife?: A Comprehensive Overview of the Evidence*, O Books, 2005

Fontana, D., *Life Beyond Death: What Should We Expect*, Watkins Publishing, 2009

Ireland-Frey, L., *Freeing the Captives: The Emerging Therapy of Treating Spirit Attachment*, Hampton Roads Publishing, 1999

Lawton, I., with Tomlinson, A.,*Wisdom of Souls*, Spiritual Rational Press, 2006

Mack, P., *Healing Deep Hurt Within; The Transformational Journey of a Young Patient Undergoing Regression Therapy*, From the Heart Press, 2011

Mack, P., *Life Changing Moments in Inner Healing*, From the Heart Press, 2012

Mayer, L., *Celestial Conversations: Healing Relationships After Death*, Cape House Books, 2012

Mongan, M., *HypnoBirthing®*, Souvenir Press, 2007

Newton, M., *Journey of Souls: Case Studies of Life Between Lives*, Llewellyn, 1994

Newton, M., *Destiny of Souls: New Case Studies of Life Between Lives*, Llewellyn, 2000

Shroder, T., *Old Souls: Compelling Evidence from Children Who Remember Past Lives*, Simon & Schuster, 2001

Stafford, B., *The Afterlife Unveiled: What the Dead are Telling Us About Their World*, O Books, 2011

Tomlinson, A., *Exploring the Eternal Soul*, From the Heart Press, 2012

Weiss, B., *Many Lives, Many Masters*, Piatkus, 1994

Weiss, B., *Only Love is Real: a Story of Soul Mates Reunited*, Piatkus, 1997

Weiss, B., *Same Soul, Many Bodies*, Piatkus, 2004

Woolger, R., *Healing Your Past Lives*, Sounds True, 2004

Regression Therapy Associations

Society of Medical Advance and Research with Regression Therapy (SMAR-RT)

This is an international group of researchers led by medical doctors who share the vision to bring about the integration of complimentary and holistic approaches into medicine. It conducts medical research using regression therapy and promotes regression therapy to the medical profession and the wider public.

Website: http://www.smar-rt.com

Spiritual Regression Therapy Association (SRTA)

This is an international association of regression and life between lives therapists that respect the spiritual nature of their clients. They are professionally trained by the Past Life Regression Academy to international standards and work to a code of ethics that respects the clients' welfare.

Website: http://www.spiritual-regression-therapy-association .com

Earth Association of Regression Therapy (EARTh)

This is an independent association with the objective to improve and enlarge the professional application of regression therapy. It provides internet forums, newsletters and professional standards for the regression therapy training schools that are recognized by it. Every summer it offers a series of workshops for ongoing professional development.

Website: http://www.earth-association.org

International Board of Regression Therapy (IBRT)

This is an independent examining and certifying board for past life therapists, researchers and training programs. Its mission is to set professional standards for regression therapists and organizations. The website has a list of international accredited past life and regression therapy training organizations.

Website: http://www.ibrt.org

About the Author

Daniela I. Norris is a former diplomat, turned writer and speaker. She currently lives with her family near Geneva, Switzerland. She invites you to visit her websites www.danielanorris.com and www.tweetsfromtheafterlife.com for more information about contact with the Other Side and upcoming events.